ART AND ARTIFICE IN SHAKESPEARE

A STUDY IN DRAMATIC CONTRAST AND ILLUSION

BY

ELMER EDGAR STOLL

> *'Tis not a lip or eye we beauty call,*
> *But the joint force and full result of all.*
> POPE

> *A legitimate poem...the parts of which mutually*
> *support and explain each other...the balance or*
> *reconcilement of opposite or discordant qualities.*
> COLERIDGE

> *For the effect of genius is not to persuade or con-*
> *vince the audience, but rather to transport them out*
> *of themselves.... The object of poetry is to enthral.*
> LONGINUS

UNIVERSITY PAPERBACK

BARNES & NOBLE • NEW YORK
Publishers • Booksellers • Since 1873

First Edition 1933
Reprinted 1934

Reprinted 1951, 1962 by Barnes & Noble, Inc.
by special arrangement with Cambridge University Press

L.C. catalogue card number: 62-12225

PRINTED IN UNITED STATES OF AMERICA

Preface

THIS book is not a reprint, with revision. But since it is, at many points, a development and organization of thoughts expressed before, I have had, as a matter of necessity, to recur to these. Of the relation of the present undertaking to the previous ones, I speak more definitely in Chapter I, p. 4; here I wish only to express my gratitude to the University of Minnesota Press for permission to make use of some material in my *Othello* (1915), *Hamlet* (1919), and *Poets and Playwrights* (1930); and the Macmillan Company, of New York, for similar permission with regard to my *Shakespeare Studies* (1927).

A still greater debt is, manifestly, owing to the publisher of the present volume, penned, on such a subject, by a foreigner. The University of Cambridge, happily, recognizes in the domain of scholarship no walls or frontiers; her Press is not reserved for her faculty or the nation; and it is a particular satisfaction to appear, under such auspices, on Shakespeare's own soil, where the dramatist has, despite my strictures, been more finely and sympathetically interpreted than anywhere else. It is there that men best speak his tongue, best hear his voice.

As an approach or introduction to the text stands an array of principles, or dogmas as I call them, from the

iii

pens of great critics. In my work I have not consciously followed them; some of them I had forgotten, others till of late I had not known; but if I should prove, after all, to have been faithful to them, I should then have the satisfaction of being, even in my heterodoxy, not unorthodox, and of not seeming to differ for heresy's sake.

Controversy in Shakespeare criticism, now after nearly two centuries of it, is, for one who would write for the mind as well as the emotions, fairly unavoidable; nevertheless I have endeavoured to avoid it save when needed to clear the way directly before me; and whatever value there may be in the book I have written lies, I think, in what is positive and constructive, poetical and dramatic, not "scientific" or "historical", as these words are, in connection with literature, abused. Here, again, it is in the light of the *Dogmata* that I would be judged—after that shed by the poet himself; and if in detecting and tracing his artifices I do not make the beauty of his art not only more credible but a little more apparent, I must, quite as much as my reader, account my labour to have been futile.

E.E.S.

Contents

CHAP. I. The Present Undertaking   1

The core of drama is not character, but situation, an effect of compression and contrast; the most striking generally secured at great cost to probability. The present writer's purpose.

CHAP. II. *Othello*   6

§ 1. The hero a prey to passions foreign (in a sense) to his nature. The convention of the calumniator credited, in this and other plays of Shakespeare. § 2. The psychological improbability in the play, by some critics now recognized. § 3. There *is* jealousy, without the predisposition; though Coleridge denied the former, and Schlegel posited the latter. § 4. The psychological improbability, price of a great contrast, made possible by an initial postulate—that Othello's mind is open and Iago's impenetrable —and made acceptable by the powerful and skilful dramatic and poetic treatment. § 5. Made acceptable above all by the creation of an illusion, through the emotional energy set free not only by the initial postulate, but by complementary, supporting fictions, or extensions of this:—that Othello's mind should *not* be thus open, and that Iago's should be closed, to others; that Iago should seem honest and sagacious to all. The case of Emilia's conduct, hitherto interpreted as stupidity or disloyalty. § 6. On the two interdependent fictive contrasts, of Iago's honesty and of Othello's jealousy, the structure of the play depends; the reconcilement of opposite or discordant qualities being in part achieved, and the emotional effect heightened, by a dramatic and poetic method that approaches the musical. § 7. A musical method in the development, but the principles of relative representation

CONTENTS

irony (until late in the eighteenth century) in the opinion
of both the public and the critics; and this opinion justified
by the text.   § 4. The tragedy cannot be both what it was
in its own day manifestly intended and understood to be,
and also what it has been taken to be of late.   § 5. By this
interpretation the feigned madness, and the hero's whole
character, particularly his reticence, are more intelligible
and appreciable.   § 6. Shakespeare himself concerned less
with minor consistency in character or story than with the
dramatic interest and illusion, the attraction of the hero
and an emotional effect. A musical method.   § 7. The
Grave-diggers' scene as an illustration.   § 8. The present
interpretation in harmony with the later opinions of Mr
Clutton-Brock.

*Romeo and Juliet; Julius Caesar; Antony and Cleopatra;
Coriolanus.*

In Comedy, ancient, Renaissance, and even the modern,
is to be found a similar artificial situation, for a corresponding purpose.

§ 1. What is lacking in modern comedy and tragedy both
is for the most part what is misapprehended in Shakespeare, the "bold strokes" and the "precipitation of
spirit", richer in effect than is realism.   § 2. Therefore the
best comic and tragic writers, like Pirandello and O'Neill,
are now falling back upon what are modern and contemporary equivalents of the outworn artifices, such as slander
and disguise. Such artifices serve an unchanging need in
drama—that of accumulation and compression, to make
us think and feel.—The still higher need in tragedy,
that of a reconciliation to life, in the moderns and in
Shakespeare.

CONTENTS

Dogmata Critica

The Importance of the Poet's Purpose

In everything the end aimed at is of prime importance.

Aristotle, *Poetics*, VI, 11 (Bywater).

A perfect Judge will read each work of Wit
With the same spirit that its author writ.

Pope, *Essay on Criticism*, l. 233.

Was hat sich der Autor vorgesetzt? Ist dieser Vorsatz
vernünftig und verständig? und inwiefern ist es gelungen, ihn
auszuführen? Werden diese Fragen einsichtig und liebevoll
beantwortet...

Goethe *Manzonis
Carmagnola* (*Werke*, Jubeläum, XXXVII, 180).

"To see the object as in itself it really is", has been justly
said to be the aim of all true criticism whatever.

Pater, *Renaissance*, Preface.

Déterminer ce qu'un auteur a voulu faire, et comment il
l'a fait, ce doit être le premier souci du critique.

Sainte-Beuve.

On peut, donc, jusqu'à un certain point, voir dans une
œuvre autre chose encore que ce qu'y a vu l'auteur, y dé-
mêler ce qu'il y a mis à son insu et ce à quoi il n'avait point
songé expressément.

Causeries du lundi, "M. Taine", 3me édition, XIII, 257.

ix

Le critique ne doit apprécier le résultat que suivànt la nature de l'effort.... Cela a été écrit déjà mille fois. Il faudra toujours le répéter. Maupassant, preface to *Pierre et Jean*.

Only, one *caveat* must be borne in mind when attempting to answer them [questions about the poet's purpose]: the poet's aim must be judged at the moment of the creative act, that is to say, by the art of the poem itself, and not by the vague ambitions which he imagines to be his real intentions before or after the creative act is achieved.

Spingarn, *Creative Criticism* (1931), p. 18.

Judge by results, I say; not by the results of reverie, which the poem merely sets going, and in which attention may ramble anywhere it pleases, for that is not criticism at all; but certainly by any result that may come of living in the art of the play and attending to everything it consists of.... But, when I say a play exists in what it means to any one who will receive it, the implication is plain, that everything is excluded from that existence which is not given by the author's technique. The existence of a work of art is completed by the recipient's *attention* to what the author says to him; whatever may come in through *inattention* to that does not belong to the art at all.

Lascelles Abercrombie, *A Plea for the Liberty of Interpreting* (1930), pp. 21, 29.

It seems to me that we should be tolerant when poets are too childlike.... But for infantilism in critics I do not see a word of defence or apology possible to be spoken.... When they are so little developed, so shut up in their own view-point, that they do not know the difference between receiving a communication and making up a fairy-story, etc.

Eastman, *The Literary Mind* (1931), p. 121.

And it [the intellectual life] leads them to see that it is their business to learn the real truth about the important men, and

things, and books, which interest the human mind....To be
satisfied with fine writing about the object of one's study, with
having it praised or blamed in accordance with one's own likes
or dislikes, with any conventional treatment of it whatever, is
at this stage of growth seen to be futile.

Arnold, *A French Critic on Milton.*

What the Purpose Is

As Tragedy is an imitation of personages better than the
ordinary man, we, in our way, should follow the example of
good portrait-painters, who reproduce the distinctive features
of a man, and, at the same time, without losing the likeness,
make him handsomer than he is.   Aristotle, *Poetics*, xv.

But from another point of view they [the impossibilities] are
justifiable, if they serve the end of poetry itself...if they make
the effect of some portion of the work more striking.

Ibid. xxv, 5.

For the effect of genius is not to persuade [or, convince] the
audience, but rather to transport them out of themselves.

Longinus, *On the Sublime*, I, 4 (Butler).

The object of poetry is to enthral [emotional illusion].

Ibid. xv, 2.

Non enim res gestæ versibus comprehendendæ sunt, quod
longe melius historici faciunt, sed per ambages deorumque ministeria et fabulosum sententiarum tormentum praecipitandus
est liber spiritus, ut potius furentis animi vaticinatio appareat
quam religiosae orationis sub testibus fides.

Petronius Arbiter, *Satyricon*, 118
(quoted admiringly by Dryden and Coleridge).

Imagination in a man or reasonable creature is supposed to participate of reason; and when that governs, as it does in the belief of fiction, reason is not destroyed, but misled, or blinded; that can prescribe to the reason, during the time of the representation, somewhat like a weak belief of what it sees and hears; and reason suffers itself to be so hoodwinked, that it may better enjoy the pleasures of the fiction.

Dryden, *Defence of Dramatic Poesy.*

'Tis not a lip or eye we beauty call,
But the joint force and full result of all.

Pope, *Essay on Criticism*, l. 245.

...yet so as to transfer from our inward nature a human interest, and a semblance of truth, sufficient to procure for these shadows of imagination that willing suspension of disbelief, for the moment, which constitutes poetic faith.

Coleridge, *Biographia Literaria*, chap. xiv.

A poem is that species of composition, which is opposed to works of science, by proposing for its *immediate* object pleasure, not truth; and from all other species— (having *this* object in common with it)—it is discriminated by proposing to itself such delight from the *whole* as is compatible with a distinct gratification from each component part. *Ibid.*

A legitimate poem...the parts of which mutually support and explain each other.... *Ibid.*

That synthetic and magical power...Imagination...reveals itself in the balance or reconcilement of opposite or discordant qualities...and, while it blends and harmonizes the natural and the artificial, still subordinates art to nature. *Ibid.*

xii

[Of a landscape of Rubens, where the light falls from opposite sides] der kühne Griff des Meisters, wodurch er auf geniale Weise an den Tag legt, dass die Kunst der natürlichen Nothwendigkeit nicht durchaus unterworfen ist, sondern ihre eigenen Gesetze hat... in den höheren Regionen des künstlerischen Verfahrens, wodurch ein Bild zum eigentlichen Bilde wird, hat er [der Künstler] ein freieres Spiel, und er darf sogar zu Fiktionen schreiten, wie Rubens in dieser Landschaft mit dem doppelten Lichte getan.

Goethe, *Gespräche mit Eckermann*, April 18, 1827.

The transcript of his sense of fact rather than the fact, as being preferable, pleasanter, more beautiful to the writer himself.   Pater, *Essay on Style*.

L'art dramatique est l'ensemble des conventions universelles ou locales, éternelles ou temporaires, à l'aide desquelles, en représentant la vie humaine sur un théâtre, on donne à un public l'illusion de la vérité.

Sarcey, *Essai d'une Esthétique de Théâtre*.

The purpose of the novelist's ingenuity is always the same; it is to give to his subject the highest relief [not the closest verisimilitude] by which it is capable of profiting.

Percy Lubbock, *The Craft of Fiction*, p. 173.

A "living" character is not necessarily "true to life". It is a person whom we can see and hear, whether he be true or false to human nature as we know it. What the creator of character needs is not so much knowledge of motives as keen sensibility; the dramatist need not understand people; but he must be exceptionally aware of them.

T. S. Eliot, *Selected Essays*, p. 188.

Chapter I

THE PRESENT UNDERTAKING

THE core of tragedy (and of comedy too, for that matter) is situation; and a situation is a character in contrast, and perhaps also in conflict, with other characters or with circumstances. We have ordinarily been taught that with the author character comes first and foremost, not only in importance but in point of time, and (cause of no little confusion) that the action is only its issue. But there is no drama until the character is conceived in a complication; and in the dramatist's mind it is so conceived at the outset. This is when the whole is invented, as nowadays it is supposed to be: when, as with the ancients and the Elizabethans, an old story was used anew, then, obviously, the plot came foremost in time and the characters were invented to fit it. And not only in those days, but in any when drama has flourished, plot—not intrigue, of course, or external activity, but situation, which is its centre of energy—has been first in importance too. Even in this era of anarchy and chaos a drama in which the characters are presented *not* in a complication, is really none. Aristotle, who by literary and psychological critics has, regretfully, been taken to task for saying it, is justified by the facts: "We maintain, therefore, that the first essential, the life and soul, so to speak, of Tragedy is the Plot; and that the characters come second.... We maintain that Tragedy is primarily an imitation of action, and that it is mainly for the sake of the action that it imitates the personal agents ".[1] And not really out of harmony with this is the subsequent precept, that "whenever such-and-such a personage says or does such-and-such a thing, it shall be the probable or necessary outcome of his character ".[2]

Unlike many critics to-day, the Stagirite did not so much explore his own opinions and sensibilities as examine the practice of dramatists, who, then as now, were so eager for a good situation that, wherever found, they seized upon it, whether new or old. And the situation they have deemed the best is that in which the contrast or conflict is sharpest and most striking, the probability or psychological reasonableness of it being a secondary consideration. Indeed, in the greatest tragedies (and comedies and epics too) the situation has been fundamentally improbable, unreasonable. What are the greatest stories in the world? Those of Orestes, Oedipus, Achilles, and Odysseus; of Iphigeneia, Dido, Phaedra, Medea, and Herod and Mariamne; of Tristram and Isolt, Siegfried and Brünnhilde; of the Cid, Faustus, and Don Juan; of Lear, Othello, Macbeth, and Hamlet: all of them embodying situations improbable to an extreme degree. Their improbability is the price of their effectiveness: such fine and fruitful situations life itself does not afford. The sharper conflict provokes the bigger passion; the more striking contrast produces the bigger effect: and to genius the improbability is only a challenge.

[1] *The Art of Poetry*, Bywater (1929), p. 38 (§ 6). In my humble but insistent justification, at this point, of the first of critics I am delighted at last to receive, whether he himself is aware or not, the support of one of the exquisites. See Bonamy Dobrée, *Restoration Tragedy* (1929), p. 33: "The conception of character being the playwright's object has vitiated, not only criticism, but also playwriting, for longer than it is agreeable to think".

[2] § 15.

In the list above Shakespeare's greatest plays are numbered; but most of the others, tragic, or comic, or even historical, are as little the sort of thing we meet in life. *Timon, Romeo and Juliet, Richard III, The Merchant of Venice, Much Ado, As You Like It, The Comedy of Errors, All's Well, Measure for Measure, Cymbeline, Pericles, The Winter's Tale, The Tempest*: these, and the greater ones already mentioned, are stories of disguise, mistaken identity, feigning, or substitution; of tyranny or trickery, deception or slander; of eavesdropping, or the fateful finding of rings, letters, or handkerchiefs; of apparent deaths and revivals; of riddling wills, vows, or oracles; of love or generosity suddenly and irrevocably turned to hatred; and of Fate or the Supernatural, villainy or magic, love or revenge, triumphant over all. These devices, as artificial and outworn, are nowadays taboo. But alike they are only the traditional means of attaining the contrast or conflict, the compression and condensation, which drama of necessity seeks. In themselves they are devices of accumulation and simplification.

Now "the impossibilities are justifiable", says Aristotle, " if they serve the end of poetry...if they make the effect of some portion of the work more striking". For, as Longinus observes after him, "the effect of genius is not to persuade [or convince] the audience but rather to transport them out of themselves;...and the object of poetry is to enthral".[1] To these primal and primordial critics, then, as not to the Shakespearean, and to the world-famous dramatists, if not, in such measure, to the modern, the whole is more important than any part, the dramatic and

[1] See "Dogmata Critica" above.

I-2

3

poetic structure than the characters, and emotional illusion than verisimilitude. And they are, I think, to Shakespeare.

    In the study of these matters in relation to him I shall for the most part keep to the tragedies; and because of the special difficulties there presented, to the four generally considered the greatest. The situation in these I have, here or there, discussed already; and I shall of necessity incur, though I have endeavoured to avert, the reproach of repetition. If only those who join the ranks of scholarship could from the outset know their appointed day! Then, however insistently and diligently they should apply themselves, they might securely refrain from print till a twelvemonth or so before it, and spare the world both repetition and revision. Not that I am myself aware of having anything to retract; I hope, indeed, that I have something of importance to add; but this I cannot present, in its due relations and proportions, without gathering up the threads and presenting the subject as a whole. In a work of art (and therefore in the interpretation) everything depends upon, and supports, everything else. To a work of art there are no additions or appendages; and to criticism, no postscripts. And here of mere repetition there is little: there is reconstruction, or adjustment, instead. What I am intent upon is the positive, not the negative, is truth, not widespread and prevailing error; ideas produced in the articles and monographs I develop, and relate anew; and the book is a synthesis of my opinions concerning Shakespeare's central structure, now put upon paper, as it has naturally (or unnaturally) come about in my mind. The subordinate structure I pass over, having recently discussed it.[1]

The study is one in dramatic art, not in dramatic evolution; and that is the reason I shall not take up the plays in chronological order. My object is to show an essentially identical method, for an essentially identical purpose, in the finest work of Shakespeare and not only of the ancients but even of some of the moderns; and I begin with *Othello* because it is the crucial case. Here, in its most complete and fruitful, but also most improbable, form, is the situation as I conceive of it; and the relation of character to action; and the supremacy of dramatic effect and illusion over both. And thereupon I show something of the same art elsewhere.

[1] *Poets and Playwrights* (1930), Chap. III, "Shakespeare and the Moderns".

Chapter II

OTHELLO

§ 1

OTHELLO and *Macbeth*, as the two wholly original tragedies—founded, that is, directly upon a story or legend, not a play—offer the clearest indication of Shakespeare's tragic conception and procedure. What of this becomes apparent may most fairly be accounted his deliberate or spontaneous choice; and in both cases it involves the sort of situation that I have been describing, as improbable and as rich in contrast as any. The hero, particularly in *Othello*, is a prey to passions foreign (in a sense) to his nature, and is led into conduct to which he is not inclined.

In my monograph,[1] years ago, I pointed out the want of any jealous, or sexually suspicious, nature in the Moor previous to the temptation; the certainty that the passion then ensuing was jealousy nevertheless; and the propriety of considering the transition from the one state to the other, without evidence for the accusation or likelihood on the face of it, to be impossible as psychology, and owing to the convention, not infrequent in tragedy and comedy, as in myth and legend, of believing at the critical moment the detrimental thing that is cunningly told. Though less obvious and external, it is an artifice of constructive character, like other traditional forms of deception in fiction, such as disguise and eavesdropping.

[1] *Othello* (1915).

6

And I showed that the use of this convention is no isolated instance in Shakespeare; being employed not only in the tragedy almost immediately preceding (or succeeding), where kindly old Gloster, without reason, and without staying for a reason, believes his ambitious bastard son, who "has been out nine years", as he slanders the earl's legitimate and favourite son, who has been at home; but also, shortly before that, in *Much Ado*, where the noble Claudio, with consequences almost as tragic, believes the sour Don John, who, he rightly thinks, loves him not, as the scoundrel slanders his sweetheart Hero; as well as afterwards, in *Cymbeline*, where the noble Posthumus, with consequences for both heroine and hero more terrible still, believes the stranger and foreigner Iachimo as he slanders Imogen. (Perhaps the most remarkable and most patently unpsychological instance is still another—that in *Macbeth*, where Malcolm repeatedly and ever more grievously slanders, not others, but himself, Macduff, in turn, with no conceivable motive or possible predisposition, credits his words, and then, on Malcolm's contradicting them, credits his words once more.) In all these cases, but most conspicuously and effectively in *Othello*, the generous and unsuspicious hero, believing a person whom he does not love or really know and has no right reason to trust, to the point of disbelieving persons whom he loves and has every reason to trust, falls, in the self-same scene, without proof of the accuser's or inquiry and investigation of his own, into a jealous rage, and resolves publicly to repudiate or secretly to kill the person suspected. And in all these cases the story told is unlikely on the face of it—how could any of the women incriminated, if to her lover not really a stranger, have been suspected, even if frail or faithless, of anything so gross and bestial as Hero's admitting the low Borachio into her chamber the night before her wedding; or as Imogen's total and unconditional surrender to the "yellow" and lascivious Iachimo at sight; or (a matter of fact here as well) as Desdemona's granting Cassio so many favours, or any, since her arrival in Cyprus, which was but yesterday? Yet the grossness—the improbability —of the charges only serves to enrage the hero the more.[1]

And this situation, in which acquaintance and evidence count for so little, is to be found, though without the denial of a suspicious or jealous nature to the hero (but also without Shakespeare's poetic and dramatic effectiveness) in other Elizabethan and Renaissance tragedies and comedies, such as *Philaster*, and even in modern ones, such as Voltaire's *Zaïre* and Schiller's *Kabale und Liebe*; and in the *Hippolytus* of Euripides and the tragedies of Seneca and Racine founded upon it; not to mention old stories like those of Joseph and Potiphar, Bellerophon and Proetus, and the various others, in divers tongues, of false stewards and malignant stepmothers. In these, certainly, it is not the image of life; and if Shakespeare's use of the convention, though vastly superior, be intended for such, is this greatly to his credit?

§ 2

I am now not quite alone in taking this sceptical but, as I think, rational, and, in the long run, poetical and dramatic, point of view. Many critics, indeed, as in the earlier

[1] This is, psychologically, on a level with Hippolito's believing that his sweet and innocent wife Infelice had compromised herself with Bryan, the Irish footman, in Dekker's *Honest Whore* (c. 1604), III, i. Like Malcolm, she had, for a purpose, brought the charge against herself.

discussion I noticed, have had misgivings concerning the psychology of Othello's transition or transformation, though with a different result. But recently Mr Granville-Barker, in considering the case of Gloster, observed that "Shakespeare asks us to allow him the fact of the deception, even as we have allowed him Lear's partition of the kingdom ".[1] That is, in all three instances, it is simply an initial postulate, and the very same in two—which, so far, is exactly what I hold. And still more recently Mr John Bailey declared that "nothing can palliate the absurdity of it. Why Edgar writes to Edmund, who is with him in the same house, why Gloster does not know his son's writing, why he accepts so clumsy a forgery as genuine, why he never insists on seeing Edgar and why Edgar never insists on seeing him, are all questions impossible to answer, yet certain to be asked, even by casual spectators in the theatre ".[2] This last objection, that the doubter and the doubted are not in frank and sober inquiry confronted, applies equally to *Othello*;[3] as well as the more fundamental one of their failure at this juncture, despite long acquaintance, to enjoy any knowledge of each other's character, or to suspect (and resent) the highly suspicious activity of the intermediary—his echoes and shrugs, questions and misgivings, feints and

[1] *Prefaces, First Series* (1927), p. 203. But Mr Granville-Barker does not keep to this point of view, and blames Gloster more than the dramatist does.

[2] *Shakespeare*, English Heritage Series, p. 173.

[3] In this play they are confronted, but only after the hero is incapable of inquiry. As in all the tragedies of jealousy (whether so-called or not)—in *Much Ado, Cymbeline,* and *The Winter's Tale,* as in Euripides' *Hippolytus* and Congreve's *Double-Dealer,* the jealous rage comes first, and the inquiry, if there be any, afterwards.

dodges, pretences and denials, and whisking of evidence under the person's nose and sticking it in his pocket.[1] An honest man who undertakes to tell you that your son—or that your wife, along with your dearest friend—has played you false, makes a clean breast of it, I suppose, without flourish or ado; and does not twist and turn, tease and tantalize, furtively cast forth the slime of slander and ostentatiously lick it up again. And certainly, though Iago's imposture is far subtler and cleverer, the situations are, psychologically and dramatically, one and the same. Indeed, the improbability here is in some regards greater, the convention more manifest. For Othello is in his prime, Gloster is old and a little maundering; Othello is explicitly and repeatedly declared not to be suspicious by nature, of Gloster in this connection nothing is said: and Othello is made to believe a man whom he has officially slighted, and with whom he is little acquainted, to the detriment of his newly wedded wife and his most intimate friend, while Gloster merely believes one son as against another. And of such aspersions and pretences, as found in either play and in life itself, the difference in effect, upon a character similarly unsuspicious and sensible, plainly appears on comparison with other great fiction (even where, as in the first of these cases, such an entanglement is by the tale-bearer desired), like *The Ring and the Book*, *Tom Jones*, and *War and Peace*. Guido's imposture, by letter or message sent to Caponsacchi as from Pompilia, or as from him to her in reply, fails of its purpose, as it should do, with either, thougn they had seen one another but once; while Honour's truthful report from

[1] For a fuller account of Iago's subtle, but (if Othello be an autonomous personality) highly questionable conduct, see the monograph, pp. 21–2.

the kitchen wins credit with her mistress only after it is confirmed by the chambermaid and Tom is found missing in his own room and bed, and that of Anatol's being a married man wins it with Natacha only after being vouched for by Peter, her friend from childhood. In two good recent plays this difference in effect appears in one and the same person, according to the mood and circumstances. In Philip Barry's *Paris Bound*, the bride herself, hearing that there has been something of a scene below, at the wedding, induces her husband to have a consolatory interview with her rival; but, six years later, takes serious and jealous notice of a friend's casual remark that she and her husband were observed, very happy together, in an out-of-the-way place on the Riviera (where he may have been but she herself was not) the year before: and in *Mourning Becomes Electra* Orin, the Orestes, is but moved to anger against his sister by her charges of murder against their mother until, by her adding those of adultery, his Freudian jealousy is awakened. But why "read authors", and neglect our wits? As mere matter of fact and logic, unless Othello and Gloster be of a jealous or suspicious nature their facile susceptibility to slander is impossible. When we stop to consider, who, save in fiction, believes or disbelieves anything, told by anybody, whether foe or friend, with or without due allowances for the teller's motives, if he be not inclined to do so?

§ 3

Now there can be no question, for those who either heed the text or hearken to critical authority, of Othello's lacking the jealous nature before temptation, and being

11

jealous thereupon without it; and only the transition causes difficulty. Though he is running counter to his source in doing so, Shakespeare has made the matter certain, not only at first hand, in the presentation of the character, but by the comment of the villain and almost everybody else in the story, the hero included; and as I have elsewhere shown, both the direct presentation and the comment, in a Shakespearean play or any other, must pass current with the audience at par. A play is not a study or a puzzle—really nowadays it is not. Only where the evidence of character and conduct is glaringly to the contrary, as with Iago's "honesty", for example, is it to be discounted. Here, on the other hand, such evidence is altogether in harmony; and even Coleridge, considering whether it be jealousy that takes possession of Othello, insists that there is no trace of such a nature in him beforehand. It is interesting and instructive to see at this point the same psychological bias diversely asserting itself, with a similar logic, but very dissimilar poetic and dramatic tact, in him and Schlegel. Again and again the English critic declares that "there is no predisposition to suspicion, which I take to be an essential term in the definition of the word".[1] Hence, indeed, his conclusion that what ensues is not jealousy, but "a belief forced upon him by Iago...an agony that the creature whom he had believed angelic...should be proved impure and worthless". Schlegel (and many of the Germans after him), recognizing that of jealousy this passion bears neverthe-less the unmistakable earmarks, is constrained to discover it slumbering in him from the outset. In either case, then, one-half, though a different one, of the dramatic presen-

[1] Raysor, *Coleridge's Shakespeare Criticism* (1931), II, 351.

12

tation is, to suit the psychological requirement, misinterpreted or ignored.

The English critic, however, being also a great poet and a dramatist, responds, despite his psychological preoccupations, far more sensitively to Shakespeare's intention. He sees the point of the comment in the play, and feels, from his first appearance, as the German cannot, the quality of the character, calm and courteous, noble and magnanimous, smiling and unruffled in the face of trouble, as, by dramatic art and the poetic at their highest potency and affinity, it is incorporated in the lines:

> 'Tis better as it is.

> The goodness of the night upon you, friends;
> What is the news?

> Keep up your bright swords, for the dew will rust them.
> Good signior, you shall more command with years
> Than with your weapons.

> Most potent, grave, and reverend signiors,
>   etc., etc.

> This only is the witchcraft I have us'd.
> Here comes the lady; let her witness it.

Othello, like most of Shakespeare's heroes and heroines, and unlike many to-day, when such artistic command over the medium is lacking, is to the spectator no disappointment, but all that his associates take him to be.

Coleridge's words above might possibly be interpreted as equivalent to our conception, but the context shows otherwise:

> Othello's *belief* not jealousy; forced upon him by Iago, and

13

such as any man would and must feel who had believed of Iago as Othello.[1]

He could not act otherwise with the lights he had.[2]

For Coleridge the situation remains psychological, actual, after all. And it is clear that the Anglo-Saxon critics, who generally have followed him, have not misunderstood his drift as they made out the tragedy (whether they denied to the passion presented the name of jealousy or not) to be one of trustfulness, not suspicion, and—here is the transition in question—to be the natural and logical outcome of the Moor's innocence and Iago's arts. The denial of its name to the passion, however, is, as Wetz asserts, only word-splitting; its being unlike that of the dramatist's Ford, Leontes, or Posthumus is simply owing to theirs being comic or (since in a comedy) having comic aspects; and as I have previously indicated,[3] it exhibits all

[1] Raysor, I, 125 (the crude and crabbed expression is owing to its being a note).

[2] Raysor, II, 351.

[3] *Othello*, pp. 10–11: "Eagerness to snatch at proofs"; "grossness of conception and a disposition to degrade the object of his passion by sensual fancies and images"; "catching occasions to ease the mind by ambiguities, equivoques, and talking to those who cannot, and are known not to be able to, understand what is said to them"; "a dread of vulgar ridicule"; and "a spirit of selfish vindictiveness". The reader need only recall the "proofs" of the dream and the handkerchief; the hero's words "lie with her and on her", "lips and noses", "goats and monkeys"; his ambiguities with Desdemona and Emilia; his dread of a cuckold's shame; and his cries for blood and his vows to tear her all to pieces, to chop her into messes, and to throw Cassio's nose to the dogs. The only difference lies in the uniformly tragic treatment of these traits, rare in the Elizabethan age, and their being suggested to a noble nature, constantly kept before us, by a villain's wiles. These arguments are all boomerangs; and the great critic is here himself a remarkable illustration of the truth upon which he is insisting—the potency of a mental predisposition, though, in his case, not that to jealousy.

the five symptoms of the malady which the greatly gifted though uncertain critic requires, but, in allegiance to his principles, would not acknowledge here.

His psychology, in the words quoted above, seems to me word-splitting as well; or rather, juggling with words, as appears more clearly in his followers. Of Mr Edward Rose (praised by Dr Furness), who holds that

> Othello has a strong and healthy mind and a vivid imagination, but they deal entirely with first impressions, with obvious facts. If he trusts a man he trusts him without the faintest shadow of reserve—

of him and others of the tradition I have said already:

> Such a mind is the reverse of strong and healthy, though this Othello's is manifestly intended to be.... A childlike simplicity and implicitness of faith, no doubt, is what Mr Rose, like many critics, German and English, is supposing; but what child, for all his inexperience of duplicity, would hesitate a moment to give the lie to the man who speaks ill of his parents or his friends? *There* is the sophism—that trustfulness precipitates one into suspicion, that, with an Iago at hand, the unsuspicious is just the one to fall utterly a prey to doubts which his heart has never known. "A man of honest, unimaginative mind", says Professor Schelling, applying to the similar Posthumus, what, with a different "psychology", had been said by Ulrici and others of Othello; "to whom Iachimo's fabricated proofs appeal, but to whom his dastardly trick is unimaginable". But Imogen's—Desdemona's—falseness is, then, imaginable! "Naïveté, a childish ignorance of the world and man", says Dr Wolff; "why should his tried and trusted Ancient deceive him?" But why should Desdemona? "Othello had no defence against it", says Mr Brooke of Iago's plot, "because he was entirely incapable of conceiving or understanding anything so ignoble". If experience—or inexperience —or nobility of soul makes him trust Iago, all the more, then,

should the one or the other, and his heart's love into the bargain, make him trust her, who had without stint or limit
trusted him. No doubt proof of the falseness of the loved one
might lead a trustful child or man to be suspicious generally;
but into suspicion Othello is precipitated, without proof. And
it is only, as I said, by means of a specious and unreal psychology that he is made incapable of distrusting the testimony
which his nature forbids him to accept, to the point of distrusting the testimony and character of those whom both his
nature and their own forbid him to discredit. "His unques-
tioning faith in Desdemona is his life", says Sir Walter
Raleigh—in so far that he immediately forsakes her and turns
wholly to Iago!¹

How often has experience taught us that even a man
whose faith is considerably less to him than life can only
with the greatest difficulty be made to believe, not (as
here) a groundless lie, but the simple truth concerning the
loved one's treason! Love for him or her, and also (what
may really be greater) for himself—indeed, well-nigh the
whole man within him—bars the way. The critical logic
and psychology displayed above are paradoxical and
fallacious. The doctrine is, that for an unsuspicious but
sensible person it is easier to hold his nearest and dearest
to be traitors than his informer a liar. The doctrine is, that
innocence inclines to a belief in guilt rather than to a
belief in innocence, and that the most trustful man is most
capable of distrust. And since no semblance of proof is
produced by the villain until after the hero has already
been excited, the psychology implies that thought and
feeling can be transferred as blood can be transfused,
without overcoming the resistance of the subject—his

¹ *Othello*, p. 33, with a few changes.

natural prepossession in favour of the known and agreeable and prejudice against the unknown and disturbing, as well as his natural fidelity to some principle or other of inquiry and judgment. It implies that a person, not "stunned", as the more conscientiously psychological Rose and Wetz would have him, nor "a goose", as, long ago, the sensible but unpoetical Rymer would have him, nor a voluntary subject in a state of hypnosis, which is all that a real and scientific psychology could make of him to-day, can, without reason, and against his rooted inclination, believe what he is told by a person whom he believes in, to the irremediable damage of persons whom he believes in far more—which, to be sure, is just about what I have been insisting upon, though not as in life (where it is supposed to be), but only (for an artistic purpose) in a tragedy or a comedy, and not as a bit of psychology, but of art. Psychology, like law, is common sense, though art itself need not be. And Coleridge, Raleigh, Bradley, and all the other great critics must know perfectly well, when not dealing with Shakespeare, that a man who is so trustful as to accept, without inquiry or reflection, an "honest" stranger's foul tale about his newly wedded wife and his friend, is suspicious just the same. (Indeed, if psychology is demanded, he had better, in drama as in reality, be kept clearer of Rymer's judgment, which is the alternative, and think and suspect for himself.) And if such a psychology be Shakespeare's, why, then, the frank and noble, strong-minded and strong-bodied Othello of the first two acts, continually recalled to us afterwards, together with the manifold testimony to the want of a jealous or angry temper within him, are in vain. He had better have been in the book what Booth, in his latter-day preconceptions, made of him on the stage, "supple and suspicious from the beginning".[1]

§ 4

They are not in vain, I am persuaded, when we accept, not thus psychologically and paradoxically, but simply and dramatically, Iago's dictum:

> The Moor is of a free and open nature
> That thinks men honest that but seem to be so,

(even to the point of not thinking honest them that are). It is the same psychological fallacy to warrant slander as in Fletcher's *Faithful Shepherdess* (written about the same time), though not accepted as plausible by the fellow-conspirator there:

> For she is of so pure an honesty
> To think, because she will not, none will lie.

(II, iii, 29.)

But sophistry, unacceptable in psychology, is ordinarily a word without meaning in poetry, that realm of illusion;[2] and this bit of the thing itself is the gate whereby we enter there. It must be taken for granted, like other dramatic artifices for the same purpose even to-day; such as a wish or a dream come true, as in *If* and *Dear Brutus*; or amnesia, as in *Siegfried*; or the transference of the scene to the other world, keeping the customs and tastes of this, as in such comedies as *The Adding-Machine* and *Green*

---

[1] Matthews and Hutton's *Celebrated Actors*, v, 72.

[2] I. A. Richards, *Principles of Criticism* (1928), pp. 272–6. Speaking of the fact that statements in poetry are not to be verified, he says: "Even when they are, on examination, frankly false, this is no defect. Unless, indeed, the obviousness of the falsity forces the reader to reactions which are incongruent or disturbing to the poem".

Pastures. It is here the indispensable preliminary to "that willing suspension of disbelief, for the moment, which constitutes poetic faith". Or, in the words of the lesser poet but more unerring critic, which Coleridge, in those quoted, is echoing, "reason suffers itself to be so hood-winked that it may better enjoy the pleasures of the fiction". Or, again, in the words (cited in the previous chapter) of a critic more unerring and unprejudiced even than Dryden, "the impossibilities are justifiable if they serve the end of poetry itself...if they make the effect of some portion of the work more striking".[1] Or, best of all, in the words (which inspired one at least of the later critics) applied to a logical fallacy of Demosthenes, whose oratory is as poetry, "in all such cases the stronger accents seem naturally to catch our ears, so that our attention is drawn from the reasoning to the enthralling effect of the imagination, and the technique is concealed in a halo of brilliance. And this effect on us is natural enough; set two forces side by side, and the stronger always borrows the virtues of the other".[2]

The trouble is, that the critics have been taking fiction for fact; that they will have no disbelief on the part of the spectator at the outset, but only belief, or if disbelief suspended, then not "for the moment" but for all time; that they turn the impossibilities into possibilities, and the poetry into prose; that their ears are caught by the weaker accents, not the stronger. They have been laboriously quibbling and hair-splitting to keep even with him who lightly manœuvred and manipulated. They have been twisting and stretching their psychology to justify him, as

[1] For these passages see above, "Dogmata Critica".
[2] Longinus, XV, 11.

2-2

he frankly, but authoritatively, adopted an initial postulate for a great dramatic effect. And what effect is that? It is one of accumulation and compression, of simplification and concentration; to which all art, and especially drama, tends. It is a more startling and passionate contrast, an accelerated movement, a more anxious expectation and more terrible outcome, and a keener and more unmingled sympathy with both hero and heroine. I do not mean the contrast between Othello innocent and noble and Iago cunning and wicked, though it of course is there; but that in the hero himself, between his love, which is native to him, and a hatred that has not (as ordinarily) been slowly and grossly bred out of it, but has sprung up full-grown at its side. There is, as there should be, a remarkable identity of tone to the hero's voice when uttering either passion; but nowhere else in drama is there a contrast so poignant as this between them, and also between what he feels and what he does, and between what he says and does since the temptation, on the one hand, and before it and after the clearing up at the end, on the other. Both before and after, Othello is probably the most noble and engaging of all the heroes of drama or of epic; and how could the effect of the intervening change have been so striking, so tragic and heart-rending, if "easily"[1]— naturally—he had become so jealous?

It is a mechanical device, to be sure, this intrusion of the villain; but there is something of the mechanical in most art, once we get to the bottom of it. It is in a fugue and in a symphony, and of much the same sort in a great fugue or symphony and a mediocre. This difference of quality lies not in the contrivance itself but in the use of it,

---

[1] v, ii. 345, "not easily jealous".

in what is thereby contrived. And that we are not going astray in finding this particular mechanism here is evident not only from its fitness to the plain meaning of the text and the nature of the character and the situation, but also from its superiority in these regards to the psychological formula offered, with its claptrap and legerdemain. The present interpretation does not at the point in question represent the image of life, but it does not pretend to do so; and is itself, I hope, true to the play and other plays, to the nature of the theatre and the capacity of the audience. The psychological interpretation, with a trust-fulness which distrusts, a belief which directly leads to disbelief (and of the wrong person in either case)—all in a healthy, discerning, and noble mind, not diseased or per-verted—is true neither to the facts of the play nor, for all its pretensions, to those of life as we know it. What does it profit us to make Shakespeare out a psychological oracle, if such be his doctrine? In order psychologically to cope with these situations, these contrasts, which we have been tracing, the critics are reduced to paradoxes or verbal mysteries generally—like Masefield's, in *Hamlet*, "All through the play there is the uneasiness of something trying to get done, something from outside life trying to get into life, but baffled always because the instrument chosen is himself a little outside life, as the wise must be"; or Clutton Brock's (among many), "It is not merely conscience but his sovereign reason that rebels, and is shaken by its own rebellion"; or Schücking's, in *Macbeth*, "He habitually suffered from fear of his own courage". If with so little of a clue the honest Elizabethan audience could be supposed to have explored the labyrinth, where, exhausted, did they arrive in the end? If they still held

21

the thread, how much they had let slip of the emotional effect, arising out of the bold change and contrast, on the way!

What, now, of the change as dramatic movement? With the playwrights of the *grand siècle*, and to some degree the moderns, it would have been largely made up of alternations of love and jealousy in the hero's bosom, and of resolves to do or not to do the deed of vengeance. There would have been less of a contrast and more of a conflict. Othello, on the other hand, once he falls into Iago's clutches, is jealous irrecoverably until the deed is done. "Dès le premier mot.", says De Broglie, "tout est dit, tout est décidé". Since the tragedy does not, like the classical French, spring directly out of the hero's and heroine's own bosoms, it is, in its development, as in its origin, not a psychological study; but it is a more vivid imaginative spectacle, is—"like the Pontic Sea"—a more irresistible dramatic current. It is a story—which is lacking in Racine; it is a series of incidents, which show different aspects of the passion, and various stages of it, along its course; it is an *emotional* development—an eclipse, then an earthquake, then an avalanche. There are five meetings with Desdemona before the death scene, at each of which Othello is continually more brutal and outrageous until the momentary last one, itself meant only to heighten this effect. "He looks gentler than he did", says Emilia; for she had not heard the words "dismiss your attendant there", referring to the encounter yet to come. And by the initial postulate adopted, the situations where he strikes her, and plays the visitor at a brothel with her, are, like his momentary sensual imaginings, and cries for blood and mutilation, not only more endurable but (poetically) more probable, are less shocking and more tragic, than if they were presented as the natural consequence, in the circumstances, of the hero's character. The great dramatic advantages of the bestial passion of jealousy are secured without the disadvantages. The contrast is sharper—is black upon white—yet the incident or the utterance does not wound our feelings. The hero carries as much of our sympathy with him as does his Lady, within that "gate of hell". *He* can cry, and not be doubted, as one naturally jealous couldn't:

> But there, where I have garner'd up my heart,
> Where either I must live or bear no life—

and again, as poignantly as if the words were notes struck upon his heartstrings:

> O thou weed,
> Who art so lovely fair and smell'st so sweet
> That the sense aches at thee, would thou hadst ne'er
> been born.

Now and then, indeed, the tension is momentarily lowered. Sometimes, particularly at the beginning of the scene, he relaxes: sometimes he holds himself in. Sometimes he is more of a gentleman again, sometimes more of a brute. And Iago (and the audience with him) is repeatedly startled by highly dramatic interruptions and revulsions —"Ha! ha! false to me?" "Villain, be sure thou prove my love a whore, be sure of it!"; or by blind appeals for sympathy and open-hearted throes of tenderness—"But yet the pity of it, Iago! O Iago, the pity of it, Iago". But nowhere does the hero really vacillate, waver, or recoil. At Desdemona's first appearance, he exclaims,

> If she be false, O, then heaven mocks itself!
> I'll not believ't;

23

but then and there he does believe it, and we have the business of the handkerchief. Never does he repent of his suspicions or cast them for more than a moment behind him; for, in his case, in keeping with this dramatic method, suspicions are convictions. Instead of the conflict and contention, oscillation[1] or fluctuation, resolve and counter-resolve, of the Racinian or Cornelian hero, there is, through all the changes, a contrast, continually reappearing, of the two feelings side by side. He is not now loving again, now jealous, but both together. There are juxtaposition and opposition instead of contention and alternation; convulsion and outcry instead of hesitation or struggle; and this very much as in ancient tragedy, the *Antigone*, the *Oedipus*, or the *Agamemnon*, and somewhat as in the situation of disguise, of Titus' and Hamlet's feigned madness, or of Macbeth's present horror of the deed which he is doing. Through the mask of Othello's hatred the eyes of his love are ever looking:

> Come, swear it, damn thyself
> Lest, being like one of Heaven, the devils themselves
> Should fear to seize thee.

Himself he hurts even more than her.

Without debate, then, or a Gallic conflict, the action is nevertheless dramatic enough; and it rushes on, sweeping hero and heroine to their doom. At the same time it carries the audience, if not the reader, over many improbabilities. These are much more numerous than has in our discussion appeared; and involve not merely coincidence, or absence of motivation, but positive contradiction in

---

[1] I use the word as Professor Bradley does (*Shakespearean Tragedy*, 1908, p. 51), in the sense of the swaying of fortune or of the hero's decision from one side to the other.

matters of time and place, and of fact or circumstance, in
the story. The common defence of the like, when really
they are admitted, is that " we are hurried so fast from the
first suspicion of Othello to his death that we have no time
to ask questions, to doubt or debate anything".[1] The
defence is meagre. It applies only when we coolly recognize
that Shakespeare was writing for the stage and not for
print, for the time, not the ages; and hold with Goethe, as
these critics do not and, consistently, cannot, that he re-
garded his drama "as a lively and changing scene, which
was to pass rapidly before the eye and ear, and that his
only interest was to be effective and significant for the
moment". And indeed this statement is inadequate. But
critics like Professors Bradley and Brandl, and like Mr
Stopford Brooke, who wrote the preceding sentence
quoted, go farther, and transform or transfigure the
numerous coincidences from the fruit of carelessness upon
the part of the poet into the work of Fate, Chance, or a
perverted world-order.[2] The last-named notion does
double service—philosophy ekes out the deficiencies in
both plot and psychology! To keep the characters the
images of life, the image of the world is distorted; and the
characters are made its offspring, as if in Balzac or Zola.

Here is sophistry again, and not the poet's. On behalf
of most of these shortcomings the swiftness of movement
may often be pleaded in extenuation, or even in justifica-

[1] Stopford Brooke, *Ten More Plays* (1913), pp. 171–5. Mr Archer and
others have said the same.

[2] A. Brandl, *Shakspere* (1894), pp. 161–2: "Der Held wäre ein Narr wenn
er es nur mit einem Iago zu thun hätte....Hinter Iago steht eine verkehrte
Weltordnung, ihr dient er als Werkzeug". The world-order is made much
of also by Mr Bradley, with great subtlety, and with great felicity, also—if
Shakespeare's plays were philosophic and psychological documents.

tion, but not to the point of adjudging them to be merits. Even in the theatre an attentive spectator or listener might well note that Desdemona has as yet had no time or chance to betray her husband's honour, and that the handkerchief with which Cassio has already been publicly wiping his beard must really be still in Iago's pocket.[1] And then he would ask questions, just as, above, Mr Bailey said that he would on witnessing Edmund's imposture. Not swiftness of movement, but the state of mind in Othello, caused by Iago's mysterious manœuvres and innuendoes, is what makes such charges actually effective with him, and therefore, dramatically, with us. This state of mind, in turn, depends on the initial postulate of thinking men honest who but seem to be so. That, first of all, has frankly and of itself to be accepted as such, for as yet the swift movement in question has scarcely begun.

The initial postulate it is, and perhaps still more (for that is but the gateway) the force and external consistency of the characterization and the magic of the poetry, which make these and other flaws acceptable. The numerous coincidences (like Othello's and Desdemona's not noticing that the precious handkerchief in question is the one she had dropped, and Bianca's arrival, in Act IV, i, precisely when wanted) may, by rapidity of action, be obscured, but not justified—unless they are in melodrama. Defects in art are not so lightly to be taken for defects in the world-order. And much the same might be said of the contradictions in time and place, which are to be found in both melodrama and cinema, to our aesthetic vexation. Yet here also is at work Shakespeare's nobler opportunism.

[1] Bradley, *Shakespearean Tragedy*, p. 182.

Having, unlike the Greeks, the whole story to present, by "short time" he gets something approaching the effect of the unities, that of concentration and immediacy; by long time (less directly and definitely indicated) the effect of slowly moving life: the two effects, on the Elizabethan undecorated stage, conspiring more happily together, as Mr Granville-Barker notices, than on ours or than (nowadays) in the closet. And in this particular play short time is needed to save Iago from justice; long time, for the plausibility of his charge. But as we shall see in *Macbeth*, though here still more than there, it is largely by the characterization and the poetry that, before and after we are entered into the world of illusion, the spell is wrought. "It is when their minds [those of the audience] are preoccupied with his personality that the actions follow as unquestionable realities", says Mr Bridges of the latter hero; or, as De Broglie said of the present play, before him, "Such are the depth and variety of the first conception that the most striking improbabilities, the most inconceivable absurdities, pass unobserved, because no one has leisure to look to the motives of the action; but to make these out to be merits is quite another matter". The critic is thinking of Othello, Desdemona, Iago, and the other characters as first we come to know them: by their living weight and the interest of their relation to each other they give momentum to the action, which carries us along.

For here poetry does not replace the "human interest and semblance of truth" that in the world of the improbable Coleridge rightly requires. The initial postulate is no charter of licence. How different is the effect of other romantic tragedy, as that of the Restoration, recently depicted by Mr Dobrée, in a critical spirit (as the reader will notice) independently in consonance with our own:

The aspect which first strikes every reader of Restoration tragedy is its unreality—not of plot or of homely detail, for all tragedy worthy of the name from the plays of Æschylus to *Faust* is unreal with respect to fact—but in the flagrant unreality of the emotions involved. The test of truth in a tragedy is to be applied, not to the facts, but to the feelings. We ask ourselves whether, placed in the situations of the people portrayed, and making allowance for their beliefs, would we [*sic*], or anybody we know, feel and behave as they do?   *Restoration Tragedy*, p. 13.

In connection with *Othello* such a question, if it arises, is quickly answered. There is nothing extravagant, or fantastic, as in "heroic tragedy". The language, however exalted, is, as is universally recognized, that of real passion; the characters, within the limits set, are, for all the liberties taken—real people. Though under the elder literary *régime*, where, as Longinus says, "we look for something greater than human",[1] they keep, even in matter of fact, within the confines of the postulate. (It is in fact, to be sure, rather than in the emotions, that reader or spectator particularly notices and is offended by the preposterous.) The hero does not, like Almanzor, do wonders and perform miracles with sword or tongue; there is no witchcraft or supernatural intervention in the story, since in the postulate there is no provision for it. At every point save that of the deception it is fairly a real Venice, a real Cyprus. And though the hero's emotions are, by the warrant given, enlarged, and the language is heightened, they are, as in Shakespeare's other great

[1] xxxvi, 4.

tragedies, **not continually** so. As Granville-Barker says
of *King Lear*, the poet "carries us into strange regions of
thought and passion, so he must at the same time hold us
by familiar things". The hero in his rage and anguish is
sublime, yet also, as the French and Spanish tragic heroes
too seldom are, often simple and human; his conduct is
that of a man, not a paladin or a monster; his speech rises
to the pitch of "Farewell the plumed troop, and the big
wars", yet, after a moment or so, descends to that of
"Nay, stay. Thou *shouldst* be honest". For our master-
dramatist, like the Master-Builder, though he raises
"castles in the air", sets them "on a secure foundation".

And the treatment makes the story plausible. Preparations, gradations, which in drama and in poetry make
almost anything plausible, are provided for the (in itself)
incredible change: Iago's confident analysis, the hero's
foreboding on the quay, another when on the very brink
of calamity—"and when I love thee not, Chaos is come
again"[1]—and, above all, his unjudicial judgment upon
Cassio. Here Othello, who hitherto, according to our
own impression and his friends' report, could never be
ruffled, gets angry with Cassio, adopts, despite prepossession in his favour, Iago's false report without
investigation, and is, in a way, "tenderly led by the nose"
already. But these preparations are dramatic, poetic, not
psychological; they arouse tragic misgivings, rather than
rational, logical expectations. And this minor improbability in Othello's conduct as governor only makes more
acceptable the similar and greater one as a husband when

---

[1] That is, "*will* come again", as in *Venus and Adonis*, l. 1020. The line
does not indicate that Othello is uncertain. If he were to lose his love, the
world would turn to chaos. See III, iii, 90 for the whole passage.

it comes. Something of the same art is employed in the
process of temptation and provocation. In all drama there
is no technique of suggestion and incitement like "honest"
Iago's; and once we have granted the premise that the
portal of the General's mind is ajar and undefended, and
his subaltern's the contrary, his cunning is almost totally
convincing. He does not approach the subject, but leads
the Moor himself to do it; and even as he retreats he advances, as he pacifies he inflames. Desdemona's conduct,
moreover, is (and naturally too) so managed by the
dramatist as only to infuriate him and to entrap her.
Brabantio had warned him, as Iago has reminded him;
and though a generous spirit, such as Othello's, does not
suspect a woman because she has eloped with him, her
insistent pleading for Cassio, and her evasions and pre-
varications, once she perceives the momentous importance
of the handkerchief, all of which really prove her purity
and innocence, disprove it in the eyes of jealous rage.
Because of her fears and inexperience she, like a child,
continually says or does the wrong thing for herself, the
right thing for the dramatist.

§ 5

Yet this is not all. For many elements go to the making
of a tragedy, as of any great work of art; and many and
diverse considerations of which he is not fully conscious
prompt the artist. Those, however, which we have been
noticing, and are yet to notice, are entirely artistic ones,
whereby he *may* have been prompted; not psychological,
philosophical, or present-day notions, which were not
within his or his spectators' purview. They have to do
with the play as a whole, not some passage or two within

it; with the actual expression, not what the dramatist is supposed to be dimly thinking of, or we have started thinking of ourselves. Only as an artist, not as a philosopher or psychologist, did he or any other dramatist ever build better than he knew; and even as such, save as he was but following tradition, he, on reflection, knew well enough (that is, could see that he was right), though possibly he was not critical—analytical—enough to explain it.[1] And what Shakespeare is here preoccupied with,

[1] I cannot again embark upon the subject of the intention of the author as the indispensable clue and guide of the spectator or reader; for what (I hope) is the last time, I have done that in an article on *The Tempest* in the *Publications of the Modern Language Association*, September, 1932. But the recent books of Mr G. W. Knight (*The Wheel of Fire*, etc.) here demand a word. He emphatically abjures this principle of criticism (which [see "Dogmata Critica" above] is not only Pope's but Aristotle's, not only Pater's but Goethe's and Sainte-Beuve's) yet calls his criticism "interpretation". Neither designation, in fact, applies. Ignoring the dramatist's intention— that is, the context— not only in the whole play but in the individual speech and sentence, he comes to such a point that words, which normally depend on one another (*videlicet*, the context) for much of their meaning, or for an indication of their particular meaning in this instance, are to him fixed and absolute, not variable, signs or symbols; and that the phrases in which Bassanio refers to the consummation of his soul's desire as "a wild of nothing, save of joy", and Theseus speaks of the poet making shapes out of "airy nothing", and Romeo bids Mercutio peace, "thou talk'st of nothing", prove to him that for Shakespeare the concepts "nothing" and "soul" are "almost interchangeable" (*Sein und Nichtsein sind dasselbe*, I dimly remember), and "both are, of course, the 'unconscious mind' of psychology" (*Wheel*, p. 283). If, then, words are so inflexibly, irresponsibly treated, imagine what is done to the play as a whole! Mr Knight has made a popular poet, writing for the stage, as dark and unintelligible as an esoteric "modernist", a Sitwell or a Hart Crane, writing for print. Below (see p. 108) I complain of Mr Clutton Brock's ignoring the conventions and traditions of drama as the author's means of communication; Mr Knight ignores as such even the words. If Mr Clutton Brock cannot or will not read Shakespeare's score, Mr Knight cannot or will not read the text. He reads the letters only, even as the "modernist" poets and prosemen often only write them.

as we have in part seen, is not primarily the image of life but an illusion, and, as its consequence, a greater emotional effect than the mere image of life can give. In a great work of art everything is reciprocal; and though our description of the means whereby the illusion is here secured is as yet incomplete, we have already seen the emotional force, set free by the initial premise, itself contributing to the illusion. But this could not take place by warrant of the premise alone. That fiction must needs be supported by others, or rather, it must be extended and confirmed. If the hero's prestige is to be safeguarded, and our sympathy irrevocably engaged, the matter of Othello's mind being open and undefended but Iago's impenetrable, involves that of the villain's seeming so, and the hero's *not* seeming so, to all the other characters, and that of Iago's reputation for superlative wisdom into the bargain.

This, once stated, is clear of itself, but that Shakespeare was of the same opinion is apparent when we turn to the relatively small matter of Emilia, who has, for some critics, been the chief mystery and puzzle. In my monograph I endeavoured to show that her failure to speak up about the handkerchief, when she saw the to-do there was about it, was not owing to stupidity[1]—that explanation (confusing art with reality) which is, by some reputable critics, in *their* preoccupation with psychology, applied to Othello also, and thereby degrades both the character and the play as a whole. As for the last point, *not*, to be

---

[1] *Othello*, pp. 40–1. Cf. Bradley (who finds her stupid), *op. cit.* pp. 215–16, 237, 239–42, and note P.—. Certainly the critic is right in denying that Emilia has suspicions, or is, as Schlegel thinks, frivolous or disloyal. For the hero's and heroine's stupidity see Brandes, Stopford Brooke, etc.

sure, in the case of Emilia, for she is only a minor figure, the waiting woman; but in hers no more than in Othello's does the explanation fit the facts. Elsewhere, as Mr Bridges likewise notices, she is astute enough, "nor was any intelligence needed". And yet if we are to keep, as the Shakespeare critics are ever doing, to psychology, stupidity is (as in the case of Othello, too) the only explanation; for fear of Iago, disloyalty to her mistress, and, above all, Schlegel's "sinful levity" are out of the question. The only one, that is to say, except deliberate violence done to the character, as in the case of Banquo, for the sake of the plot. But why, then, was she present at the inquiry concerning the handkerchief, why was the improbability thus exposed? "The point of her presence", says Mr Bridges, "can only be to increase the tension of the spectators' anxiety: they expect her every moment to explain the mistake, and rescue Desdemona; yet she does not."[1] And, may I add, this effect, while I do not think it the "only" one (otherwise the play would here be melodrama) is continued, and greatly heightened, by Emilia's three times surmising, once in the presence of Othello and twice in that of Desdemona and of Iago himself, summoned by her in her anguish, that some "wretch"—"some busy and insinuating rogue...to get some office"—"some base notorious knave"—has put the notion of the lady's treachery into the general's head.[2] Also, the effect is one of irony, Emilia being repeatedly so near and yet so far. It is like that of Othello himself, time and again, when kept from doubting Iago by the thought of his "honesty". But it is like this for a further,

---

[1] See below, p. 42, note.
[2] Act IV, sc. ii, ll. 15, 130 ff., 140.

a higher and wider, purpose. Neither plot nor tension is the main thing here: the handkerchief might have been found by Iago without his wife's knowledge, and for tightening the tension the still unavoidable effect of stupidity is a big price to pay. There is no such price to pay. Really Emilia's want of perception is like that of Othello, Desdemona, Cassio, and everybody else in the tragedy but Roderigo, who is a confidant and tool; and more than that of any other minor character in the tragedy the obtuseness of Iago's wife supports and enforces the fiction of the impenetrableness of his mask. Emilia is not stupid since the others aren't—where would be the irony if they were?—and they themselves aren't because she isn't; and here it is chiefly a matter, not of plot, or of tension, or even of irony for itself alone, and still less of psychological defect or delusion, but of a dramatic illusion.

In all these cases, and therefore as a whole, the irony is to be felt only in the house, not on the stage. And it is quite in keeping with this conduct of hers, and also (the fiction being allowed for) with her character, and, indeed, to serve this ulterior purpose of supporting the fiction, that, upon Othello's disclosures after the murder, she gasps out, "my husband!" three times over. Now she is opening her ears and eyes as well as her mouth; for the end is at hand. Up to this moment the very yokemate of the Ancient (who is called "honest" more than a score of times, by not only Othello but Desdemona, Cassio, and even himself) cannot be permitted to suspect him, faithful and alarmed though she is. No one can be, or the colossal fiction will collapse. No one can be, or everyone else will then seem truly stupid in comparison. For upon this "exceeding honesty" the success of the intrigue, upon

34

victims and audience alike, depends, never endangered (as
in life it would be) by the question whether the honest
fellow be not, in his charges, mistaken, or by the recollec-
tion of Cassio's or Desdemona's character as to the hero
it is known. What Cassio has been to him he now has no
thought for; and Desdemona—under the Ancient's suggestion, "she's the worse for all this". Moreover, mistaken
Iago in Othello's eyes cannot be, for in sagacity he
excels as in sincerity. From the beginning of the temptation the general looks up to him, nay, from the moment of
the inquiry into Cassio's drunken misbehaviour; when
first left alone he considers that the fellow "knows all
qualities, with a learn'd spirit of human dealings"; and
when, again in leading-strings, he cries, "O thou art wise,
'tis certain". Certain it is (though in another sense) to us
as well; and all depends upon the mask, as when (though
now with explanations needed) Satan deceives the arch-
angel Uriel,

> For neither man nor angel can discern
> Hypocrisy, the only evil that walks
> Invisible except to God alone;

and when Congreve's Maskwell counts upon "dear dis-
simulation as the only art not to be known from nature".[1]
Archangels and Restoration wits must not be dupes, as,

[1] *The Double Dealer*, II, i. To be of most avail this postulate should have
appeared earlier in the play, like Iago's less explicit "And what's he, then,
that says I play the villain?" etc., before the Temptation begins. Maskwell
adopts much of Iago's policy and strategy, with the ingenious improvement
upon Iago's apparent honesty of telling his victims pretty much what he is
doing or intending to do. But his deceiving others ought to alarm his confidants for themselves, his officious activity ought to seem as suspicious as
Iago's own, and for the audience the illusion is broken by Careless' penetrating the villain's mask from the outset. In Congreve's own day Mellefont

3-2

35

without this precaution (or else Shakespeare's device of unanimity) they would be. For the same reason, in advance of the Moor, not only Roderigo but Cassio looks to "that demi-devil" for guidance. And for the same reason (as well as for the irony again) Desdemona does so unlikely a thing as to summon to her chamber, through Emilia herself, the flinty-hearted Ancient when she is heart-broken. That makes the magic ring about the stage complete: how could, then, Othello, either—"O Iago, the pity of it, Iago!"—have seen him as he is? and Emilia's whole conduct, not a puzzle, nor a flaw, is an indispensable component, not of the plot, but of the illusion.

In short, the action beginning with an improbable fiction, the fiction, to be probable, must be sustained. It is as in *Macbeth*. When Macduff believes Malcolm as he brings the heinous charges, one after the other, against himself, he must believe him still as he disavows them, or seem to have been a dupe or gull (as in real life he would be) in the first place. It is as in *Cymbeline*. Imogen and Posthumus, too, otherwise so clever and charming, have been taken (in round terms) for fools even by Mr Granville-Barker; and Iachimo, otherwise so subtle and dexterous, has been taken, in his abrupt indecent proposals to the lady, for a crass blunderer. But in Shakespeare's text, in Shakespeare's intention, and (so far as we accept his conventions and simplifications) in Shakespeare's effect on the audience, these four improbabilities—the wager; the slander of Posthumus to Imo-

was taken for a "gull"; and in the Epistle Dedicatory the author must explain that Careless' warning to him was meant simply "to give the audience some light into the villain's character before his appearance". Shakespeare manages better, by soliloquy, as if, until the end, no one could possibly know Iago but his Maker.

gen, proposal of revenge, and successful denial of both; the proposal to take the trunk into her bedchamber; and the circumstantial slander of Imogen on his return—all four, I say, hang or fall together. Why shouldn't Imogen believe Iachimo if Posthumus can make such a wager and give him a letter of introduction? If she can believe a man slandering her husband whom an hour before she has never seen, why shouldn't she believe him when he declares it was only an *essai de vertu* and praises him again? If she can then believe him anew, why shouldn't she frankly and trustfully receive his treasure into her chamber? And if Posthumus has been willing to let his belief in his wife hinge upon the evidence of conquest which Iachimo is to bring back with him, what more can he ask than the bracelet in the seducer's hand and the description of her chamber and her person upon his lips? In the play it is a little and separate world of imposture; and if one of the two so-called "fools" refused belief the structure of it would topple, and the other would be a fool indeed. Now in *Cymbeline* and *Othello* alike this world is near enough to our own, where also imposture is (within narrower limits) successful, to make us feel, where it is successful with all concerned, as if these were not foolish, and itself were not what we ordinarily think of as imposture at all.[1] The situation is somewhat similar to that

---

[1] Some critics have been of the opinion that in *Much Ado* there is irony in the circumstance that the conspiracy against Hero should have been proof against the sharp wits of the leading characters but have been laid bare by the stupid constables. This is one of the many ironies (see below, p. 128–9) without warrant in the text; the constables only stumble on the truth, overhearing instead of discovering it, and then scarcely knowing what to do with it; and not by the dramatist, as by the critics, is the reputation of Benedick and Beatrice, Don Pedro and Claudio impaired.

in *Gulliver's Travels*. The countries of Laputa and of Brobdingnag are kept like the real world, but perfectly distinct and in themselves consistent. In the one everything is in size proportionately reduced, in the other everything is proportionately exalted. Swift's imagination, says M. Hazard, "part d'une hypothèse invraisemblable, mais la maintient avec une si parfaite logique qu'elle donne l'impression du cohérent et presque du vrai".[1] For consistency in impractical fiction, even as in the practical, in the unmoral as in the immoral, is the better part of verisimilitude.

But not the whole of it; the improbable itself must be motivated, and, as Aristotle declares, be made probable; even in the world of illusion the cause must be equal to the effect; and would not, after all, the very associates of Othello at Cyprus be in danger of seeming a little gullible did not the Ancient wear his mask so well? His intrusive activity, I have remarked above, might have been suspected; but the Moor is swayed by his Ancient's reputation, which, we notice, his habitual bearing warrants. He seems honest, as a frank, blunt, friendly, and none too godly man of the world. He does not, in the circumstances of the fiction, overdo. (Indeed, some of the critics have been as much taken in by him as the people on the stage; a sensible American even called him a prince of good fellows, and thought he would not, had it kept out of his way, have trod upon a worm; and every now and then, in the conjuring game of criticism, something of this monstrous misconception is revived.) Thus Iago himself supports the fiction, imparts reality to the illusion, just as Shakespeare's heroes and heroines, both in this play and

[1] *Nouvelles littéraires*, Sept. 12, 1931.

in others, lend, by their manifest qualities or charms, credibility to the praise or passion of their admirers, and Ibsen's and O'Neill's do not.[1] And artfully honest, Lamb would have him played. Of Bensley he says:

> His Iago was the only endurable one which I remember to have seen. No spectator from his action could divine more of his artifice than Othello was supposed to do. His confessions in soliloquy alone put you in possession of the mystery. There were no by-intimations...not a man setting his wits at a child, and winking all the while at other children who are mightily pleased at being let into the secret; but a consummate villain entrapping a noble nature into toils, against which no discernment was available, where the manner was as fathomless as the purpose seemed dark, and without motive.

On the head of Iago's intellectual gifts the critics have been divided—some thinking them supreme, others limited. Some dwell on his uniform success; others, noting the prodigious risks he ran and his final failure, call it luck; both parties alike treating him as if an authenticated case, and the play as if a chapter of his "life-story". Out in the world any man whose reputation for honesty and wisdom was so complete and spotless should, for this very reason, have been a little questionable, like that of the bank-cashier-Sunday-school-superintendents in small undefended towns a generation ago. But the mere illusion, on the stage, has by the dramatist been achieved as skilfully in regard to wisdom as to honesty: every one there explicitly or implicitly acknowledges it. And in the theatre he achieves the corresponding effect, of knavish craftiness, not only by Iago's success (whether in his own playing or in pulling the strings for the puppets), but also

[1] Cf. *Poets and Playwrights*, pp. 125–6. See also above, p. 13.

(which is still more important) by his manifest superiority in thought and speech. There is witchcraft, though not like the poet's own, in his lips. His art is the black, and the ritual, of woven paces and waving hands, is in his lines.

No one like Shakespeare in *Othello* has created and preserved the illusion of delusion; and that is the reason he has taken such pains to deny his hero the jealous nature. Thereby he derives from the initial fiction its full dramatic advantage and virtue: by giving the Moor the "predisposition", making the character more psychological and the situation more probable, he would be throwing much of this away. Some of the critics who find the improbability, not in the mere change within the hero, but in the fact that Desdemona has had no time or opportunity to be unfaithful, have shown how easily it could have been provided. She and Emilia might have made the voyage with Cassio instead of Iago. But Shakespeare who, of course, and rightly, does not raise the question, will no more give Othello evidence or justification for suspicion than the predisposition itself. By the impenetrableness of Iago's mask he can have a hero who has nothing in him of the simpleton or gull; by the want of a suspicious nature he can have a hero who is wholly noble and lovable. Thus he achieves a greater complication—a generous nature in a jealous rage. Thus he can call forth and hold our sympathies for the hero in still greater measure than for the heroine; as Beaumont and Fletcher in *Philaster*, and Voltaire in *Zaïre*, and Schiller in *Kabale und Liebe* (who make the hero's hearkening to slander psychologically, though not poetically, more plausible) cannot. (But why go so far afield?—beyond the dramatist himself, somewhat neglecting his own example, in *Cymbeline*.) The end—the enormous emotional effect—justifies the means; but means and end and the whole inner substance of the play—Othello and Iago, Desdemona, Emilia and the rest of the characters, in their points of view and reciprocal relations—hang, as they should, together.

Not so the hero's character, however, save as we accept the postulate: but then, to a degree not attained in any other tragedy, he both remains himself and suffers an eclipse. Here again there is repetition, not merely as the hero at last emerges, but in the comment. Why does not Shakespeare content himself with the simple contrast of Othello serene and noble at the beginning and (though broken) at the end, and Othello jealous and furious in between? By the Elizabethan audience the words about jealousy of Desdemona and Emilia, Lodovico and Iago, and the Moor himself, were doubtless not needed (sorely as they are by the critics) for the guidance of their minds, but only of their emotions; and they are designed mainly to direct attention to the tragic change. And why from the outset does the dramatist make nearly every character but the villain unreservedly love and admire the hero as well as the heroine, and these speak and act in such a way that the audience does too? Instead of bridging the gap, he widens it, and points to it, careful still, not for the psychology, but the immediate effect; and the wonder and dismay, felt on every hand, is not only a note of reality but a stroke of emphasis, both of which make the contrast count. Desdemona's remark about the handkerchief before Othello's entry, that, save for the fact that he is "made of no such baseness as jealous creatures are, it were enough to put him to ill thinking";[1] Emilia's question upon his exit, "Is not this man jealous?" and Desdemona's bewildered reply; Lodovico's "Is this the noble Moor whom our full Senate call all in all sufficient?" Iago's headshake in answer, and Othello's own "not easily jealous" at the close—all these throw the intervening situation, which intrinsically deserves it, into high relief. And though by Shakespeare's art he is (as we have seen and are yet to see) in a manner still kept before us, we painfully miss the hero, and vividly recall him (while Lodovico continues), as he was:

> Is this the nature
> Whom passion could not shake? whose solid virtue
> The shot of accident nor dart of chance
> Could neither graze nor pierce?

The irony is that of fact, not of fact and opinion: these minor characters, in noting the change, are as right as a Greek chorus. The villain, as often in Elizabethan tragedy, takes the place of the ancient Fate: and these repeated personal reactions bring the irony home. The villain, by all this contriving of the poet's, bears in this instance, like the ancient Fate or intruding god, the burden of responsibility; and our sympathy with a hero made of no such baseness is almost without alloy.

Not that it is *without* alloy; or that Othello is less than a truly tragic figure, or fails of the *hamartia* (not a "fault" but an "error of judgment"), expected of him by Aristotle.[2] In taking full advantage of the fiction, and putting jealousy

---

[1] This, on a smaller scale, is like Emilia's inability to doubt Iago—it lends plausibility to Othello's conduct when he enters. She is of the same mind as her lord about the momentousness and suspiciousness of the loss of a handkerchief, though the husbands and wives that we know of are not.

[2] See below, p. 58, note.

upon the hero instead of breeding it in him, the dramatist nevertheless arouses within us not only pity but fear. He does not free him of blame, least of all at the end, in his own opinion; and no one in Shakespeare's tragedies more bitterly and wildly reproaches himself. He has hearkened unto Iago—like the base Indian he has thrown his pearl away; and (though "all unused") weeping and lamenting, he knows not where to turn. "Where should Othello go?" Yet not of himself suspicious or sensual, he is now not corrupted or degraded; and amid his misery and remorse, he still can hold up his head, and declare:

> For nought I did in hate, but all in honour.

> not easily jealous, but, being wrought,
> Perplex'd in the extreme.

He is a more effective tragic figure because he can say that—because, unlike many, he keeps our sympathy and admiration to the end.

§ 6

Iago honest, Othello jealous; the one predicate made on the stage a matter of course, the other an occasion for grief and wonder—these interlocking, interdependent contrasts form the inner structure of the play. And thus it fulfils the requirements of Coleridge's definition of a poem as a work of the imagination—"the balance or reconcilement of opposite and discordant qualities...the parts of which mutually support and explain each other".[1] The definition applies to dramatic poetry as to the lyric (for between them there is, as Mr Drinkwater says, no essential difference), and for that matter to other art as well, verbal or not. Is it not at bottom the same principle

[1] See above, "Dogmata Critica".

of contrast and reconcilement, thrust and counter-thrust, emphasis and subordination, interrelation and interdependence, in a drama as in an epic or lyric, a temple or a symphony, in short, the time-honoured principle of harmony and equilibrium, but in the manifestation or application ever different and new?

Indeed, as for the specimen of dramatic art before us, the various repetition, whereby the contrasts are enforced and impressed upon us, is a sort of artistic manipulation, which, overriding the ordinary restrictions of psychology and realism verges upon the confines of another art, that of music. (It is still dramatic, however, in that it serves to heighten the effect of opposition and simplification, though it lowers that of verisimilitude.) And it mingles and conspires with other musical tendencies. As in most of the great tragedies, every character has his rhythm—the hero and the villain, the heroine and her waiting-woman—and every scene, as well as the whole, has (of another sort) its own. But here there is a kind of musical method even in the presentation of the character of the hero in his changes—serene and noble at the outset, then jealous and furious, then, for all his misery, himself again. Amid his rage, as has been noticed, his love is ever before him; of his old self we are, not only by his accent and manner and by others' comments, but also by the very quality of his rage, continually reminded;[1] by a great

---

[1] See the passages quoted above, pp. 23, 43. And there are many others, in which the accent and rhythm are unmistakable, such as:

> For she had eyes, and chose me. III, iii, 189.

> No, not much mov'd.
> I do not think but Desdemona's honest. iii, 224.

And if, with such provocation, Othello, as we knew him, could really rage, no doubt he would do it after this large and imaginative fashion. Poetically

stroke of theatrical, but well-nigh musical art, it is, in the soliloquy, summoned up before us at the beginning of the murder scene; and at "Nay, stare not, masters, it is true indeed", the old Othello returns, with all his dignity (though not his serenity) upon his head, to hold and keep the stage. He has again the voice, the expanse of spirit, that captured our imagination in the Council-Chamber. Here, in the *finale*, moreover, this effect of rhythm and recurrence is appropriately heightened and intensified, as now, without psychological impropriety, and with a dramatic suspense, thoughts of the sword, the past, the future, come and go, or rise and fall, by a sort of undulation, in his consciousness.

Suicide itself ends the speech, but in that there is for us no mere surprise or empty shock of horror. Over his brain memory holds sway, as with the dying: he looks backward, even as he looks forward, to the memory that there will be of him. Though no one sees his dagger, his words breathe quiet desperation and farewell. But the point is that with delicate and various repetition and retardation of the theme, whether by the business of the sword, or hints of suicide, or reminiscences and anticipations in digression, the poet had made it apparent already that this was his "journey's end", his "utmost sail", and, as if it were in music, had prepared and reconciled our souls. And the chief point of all is that this whole final movement is an echo or reflux of that with which the play began. For here in his misery is Othello again as first we knew and loved him—in his pride, in his tenderness, even in his calm—though now by passion shaken and by the dart of chance pierced.[1]

he is still identical—"the Pontic Sea", "the error of the moon, which comes more nearer earth than she was wont and makes men mad", "aspics' tongues", and the Sibyl "in her prophetic fury", are not out of keeping with "these nine moons wasted" and "antres vast and deserts idle" (*Othello*, pp. 59–60).

[1] *Othello*, p. 61.

I wonder if Stendhal, a subtle critic, was not groping for a phrase to fit something of the same impression, as he penned the words quoted in scorn by Gourmont,

Je défie tous les classiques du monde de tirer de Racine un ballet comme le *sublime ballet d'Othello*.[1]

The unanimity, then, with regard to the honesty of Iago and the change in Othello, lends to the fiction illusion; the musical treatment, both in the *finale* and in the development of the whole tragedy, heightens this; the poetical creation of the characters gives it life and substance; and thus—and who knows how otherwise?—the audience is laid deep under a spell. It is not reality as we know it, but a "higher reality",[2] which, despite our reason, we are led to accept. All art aspires to the condition of music; at the pinnacle of its kind, as in *Othello*, stern and solid tragedy itself, though still of course remotely, somewhat approaches this; and it is not, as has been said, the swiftness of the story on the stage, but the potent harmony, not only, as here, in the structure, but also in the words, which are as notes to be sung, that (together, of course, with the "human interest and semblance of truth") stills our scruples and misgivings, and "procures for these shadows of imagination that willing suspension of disbelief, for the moment, which constitutes poetic faith". We believe, not as convinced, but as enchanted and enthralled. "I conclude", says Mr Bridges in connection with Emilia's silence, "that Shakespeare aimed at exciting his audience to the limit of endurance"; but this sort of excitement,

[1] *Promenades littéraires* (1913), ii, 101.
[2] Goethe's phrase, used by Professor Frye; but the idea, of course, is Aristotle's.

allayed (or exalted) by harmony, we can endure. And an Elizabethan audience, more accustomed to the convention, more penetrable to poetry, or less insistent upon psychology, yielded to the spell more spontaneously and appropriately than we can. There is the critic's story of the sympathetic young woman in the gallery, who stood up and cried, "You big black fool, you, can't you see?" And for all his rare and exquisite susceptibility to poetry, Mr Bridges, whether he recognizes the convention or not, seems to be responding to it over-little (or over-much) himself as, with his rare but wonted candour, he declares, "Exasperation is the word that I should choose to express the state of feeling which the reading of *Othello* induces in me". That, certainly, was not the poet's purpose; that, as certainly, was not then, and is not now, its proper effect. And that the Laureate thinks it such is owing to his clear realization of the price the poet has paid, not of all the rich domain he has purchased.

§ 7

A musical method is, once the tragedy is under way, employed in the development of it; but the principles on which it is planned appear more clearly when we turn to a more mimetic art, like painting. Not in any special sense pictorial at all, it is penned in the spirit of deft relativity and bold compromise, not foreign to both that art and poetry, but more easily discernible and more openly acknowledged there. As if it were a painting it reproduces, not facts but values, not truth but appearances, not reality but the relations of persons and things. Chiaroscuro and perspective are false in detail that they may be true as a whole. The tones of nature are in

47

painting all lowered, because the highest in painting cannot approach the highest in nature. The lines of a perfect
cube, when presented on canvas, are no longer equal. And
apart from these primary adjustments there are others
more optional and less imitable; such as the painting of
snow not white but yellow and purple to secure the effect
of radiation, or the direct apposition of complementary
colours to secure the effect of volume. And a master of
the art, a Shakespeare on canvas like Rubens, may, for a
purpose, go so far as he does in the landscape noticed
by Goethe, in the "Dogmata Critica", above, and let the
light fall from opposite directions, "proceeding even to
fictions", like the prince of dramatists in the play. His
picture, of course, is moving. But there is a Rembrandtian
concentration of light—of the interest—upon the hero, a
dramatic instead of electric spotlight focused on him, even
when he passes under the cloud of jealous fury; and as his
free soul, thus shadowed, at last shines forth again, still
himself though changed and shaken, there is such an effect,
heightened by music, as the theatre had not known or
was again to know, too simplified and striking to be true,
though not too untrue to be striking.

The trouble with Shakespeare criticism, as we have
already noticed, is that it has been prompted and guided
by the spirit of literalism. The play has been thought to
be a psychological document, not primarily a play, a
structure, both interdependent and independent, the parts
mutually, and sufficiently, supporting and explaining each
other; and the characters have been taken for the sepa-
rable copies of reality. At bottom the mistake is the same
as that of the actors, who, as Heine said, were in his day
concerned only for the characterization, "not at all for the

poetry, and still less for the art".[1] But if one character be so interpreted the others must be; if Othello is a study in psychology and tragic error, then not only he but nearly everybody else in the play must be stupid, and Emilia must be either stupid or disloyal, or else, indeed, a prey to an abrupt and disenchanting intrusion of the plot. And then her conduct is not probable; whereas by our interpretation it is, that is (in Croce's sense of the word) *coherent*, in harmony with the whole. How much finer in the poet, and more satisfying to the imagination, that the characters, one and all, should thus be deftly transported into another world, and made subject to the high and all-prevailing purpose of a tragic illusion; and that the play should be, not a transcript of fact, but, as Pater says, of the poet's sense of fact—not a cluster of studies embedded in a story, but a new creation and an individual, unbroken whole! And in so saying we are not speaking in riddles or trafficking in mysteries, but heeding the highest critical wisdom of the ages. Longinus is writing in the spirit of Aristotle before him, and of Dryden and Coleridge, Goethe and Sarcey after him, as he declares that "the effect of genius is not to persuade [or convince] an audience but rather to transport them out of themselves"; and "that the object of poetry is to enthral", is emotional illusion.[2] And perfectly in keeping with the conception of *Othello* and other great drama that we have been presenting, dramatic art has, by the last-named critic, been defined as "l'ensemble des conventions...à l'aide desquelles, en représentant la vie humaine sur un théâtre, on donne à un public l'illusion [only that!] de la vérité".

[1] *Shakespeares Mädchen und Frauen, Werke* (Bib. Inst.) v, 388.
[2] See, above, the "Dogmata Critica".

§ 8

In discovering such all-subduing unity and harmony in this tragedy (and presently in the others too) I may, to be sure, seem to be contradicting myself, in view of the looseness of texture and inconsistency of statement in Shakespeare's work that I have noticed both here and elsewhere. I have remarked upon incongruities in matters of fact and detail, time and place, character and conduct; and in fairly equal number they are to be found in many others of the plays, even his greatest.[1] Shakespeare is the least correct and punctilious of great dramatists. And unity is lacking, if we are thinking of the formal. Shakespeare's is not so much of form and structure, logic and order, as of the embracing and pervading, animating and (as we have seen) compelling spirit. It depends on inclusion rather than exclusion. For his artistic virtues are positive, opulent, redundant, not negative or corrective, frugal or austere. His motto is not the Hellenic "Nothing too much", but rather the Gothic "Nothing too little". His vices, like his virtues, are those of exuberance—there are phrases, speeches, characters, even scenes (like the Clown's in the present tragedy, and Hamlet's talk about theatrical art with the Players), which might happily be dispensed with; and how a Ben Jonson or a Racine, if fairly given the chance, would have applied, not the blue pencil only, but the shears! His very characters, as we have seen and are yet to see, often rise up out of the situation and overshadow it, are not, as in most great drama,

---

[1] Cf. Bradley, pp. 256–9 (*King Lear*), p. 73 (*Othello*); and there are the notorious cases of Cassio's wife and Lady Macbeth's children.

part and parcel of it: even by those critics who would not admit this they are (though mainly for their psychological significance) commonly considered worth far more than the rest of the play. But whether so or not, they are, as we have noticed, not independent of the play, and, save as in it, cannot be rightly interpreted. The plot is not so much a part of them as they are parts of the plot; and the converse conception has, as we have noticed, been a fundamental cause of critical trouble. And that upon the imaginative, the emotional, though not the strictly logical, consistency and coherence of the whole, Shakespeare, for all his rapidity and apparent recklessness, was intent, is apparent not only from his various measures to establish and preserve the illusion, such as the manœuvring, and hedging, and musical manipulation, which we have been discussing, but also from those artistic expedients which we have only touched upon—the atmosphere created by means of a characteristic language and imagery, and the ebb and flow in the intensity of the action, and in the metrical movement from speech to speech and scene to scene. "C'est par le rythme, dit Frédéric Lefèvre, que l'écrivain cesse d'être artisan pour devenir sorcier."[1] The atmosphere, as created and preserved throughout the play, has been best analysed by Professor Bradley, as he notes the prominence of figures in *King Lear* which have to do with wild and ravening animals, or of darkness and the colour of blood in *Macbeth*.[2] The "orchestration" of the verse and the "pattern" of the action have been best analysed by Mr Granville-Barker, as in *King Lear* and *Antony and Cleopatra*. The identity of tone and continuity

[1] *Nouvelles littéraires*, Sept. 19, 1931, p. 8.
[2] *Shakespearean Tragedy*, pp. 267–8, 333–6.

4-2

of rhythm in the single character I myself have before this [1] endeavoured to present in the cases of Cleopatra, Othello, and Iago. And is not this the unity that was to be expected of Shakespeare? This may be achieved without continual cutting and pruning—instinctively, under the mere pressure, as the pen moves, of a single, irresistible conception. It is the primary matter of the identity or continuity of stroke or touch, or of fabric and texture, and of the mood and vision behind them; rather than the secondary one of closeness and nicety of weave, of painstaking, intellectually (instead of imaginatively) economical, arrangement and elaboration. Still more, it is the matter of the inexhaustibleness of genius, satisfying the expectations it has aroused, completing what it has undertaken, as in the making of a hero, a heroine, and a villain, who in speech and demeanour, bear out all that their friends and admirers say. Shakespeare can keep his word and honour his signature—has both the imagination to conceive the thing in its fullness and the hand to fashion it. This is the unity of the *Divine Comedy*, with its rounded realization, its manifold and flexible contrasts and interplay, rather than that of *Paradise Lost*, with its noble and solid but precise and rigorous structure.[2] It is the unity of *Clarissa* (for all Shakespeare's Fielding-like vigour and variety) rather than of *Tom Jones*. It is unity of the highest, if not the most faultless, sort—that which depends on the informing spirit, ever present, an illusion never broken.

One point touched on in the preceding paragraph may

---

[1] *Poets and Playwrights*, the essay on Cleopatra; pp. 128-9 for Iago; and *Othello*, pp. 59-60.

[2] See *Poets and Playwrights*, essay on "Milton, Puritan of the Seventeenth Century", pp. 281 *et seq.*

need for a moment to be dwelt upon. Psychology and character-drawing, I have in the previous discussion taken for granted, are not one and the same. Critics so diverse as William Archer, T. S. Eliot, and A. Clutton-Brock have recognized this; and I need not now insist upon it. The psychology is the framework, so to speak; the character is the life and soul. The psychology is the anatomy; and as a great sculptor or painter may, for his purposes, here or there neglect or simplify the latter, so a great dramatist or novelist may, for his purposes, here or there neglect or simplify the former. Why should not the dramatist, like Shakespeare, have his story, his situation, his rhythm, if the painter, like El Greco, or the sculptor, like Bourdelle, must, after his fashion, have his rhythm too, even at a cost? From the absolute point of view this is a defect; but when for the whole some hitherto unsuspected beauty is thereby attained, we are reminded that all art is a compromise and the absolute point of view does not apply. And particularly is this the case with Shakespeare's characters, which, often superior to the action, or somewhat apart from it, appear to us most clearly, not in what they do or fail to do, notice or fail to notice, but, as with Othello, Desdemona, and Emilia, in what they feel and say, and in the individual accent wherewith they say it. There they are so vivid and consistent as to leave no doubt of the artistic success. It is only in characters in which the psychology is intentionally more prominent and important, and the individuality of the emotion and the identity of utterance are less signal and authoritative, as in Racine or Alfieri, that such a defect can be more nearly fatal. Or in a modern novel, where is no such necessity as in the drama to achieve condensation, and psychology is peremptorily expected and avowedly offered; and in Wassermann's *Goose-Man* it is a grave and disillusioning error that the hideous and malicious, depraved and degenerate cousin Philippina, whom the musician and his family all fear and distrust, should, with so little reason, be suffered, as servant and nurse, to obtain a permanent footing in the household. She is there for the situation, in a time when, for that, in the freer form of the novel, the prerequisites are more exacting; and the situation achieved is not significant enough to make amends. *This* is the place for exasperation.

§ 9

In *Othello*, however, there is room or occasion only for tragic delight. An established convention, when not outworn, has, even in these uncompromising days, an advantage over an invention, like that of Wassermann above, or that in Melville's fine story of Benito Cereno (where a Yankee sea captain in slave-trade times boards so suspicious a craft as the *San Dominick*, and, amid all his misgivings, fails to seize the next opportunity to get away)—the advantage of not provoking criticism, not arousing resistance. The spectator here accepts the convention without hesitation, as, even after two thousand years of use, the reader does the pastoral for elegy, in *Thyrsis* and *Ave Atque Vale*, when treated anew by a master hand. So treated that in *Othello*, of course, is. The passions are tense, the dramatic interest is engrossing. And in the highest aesthetic sense the characters are real —they are lovable or fascinating. Where in any tragedy, in any tongue, are there people who, throughout, speak more distinctly and unmistakably than Othello and Iago,

Desdemona and Emilia, Brabantio, Cassio, and Roderigo? or more penetratingly and unforgettably than the Moor, his gentle Lady, and his Ancient? "With truer accents than in Othello", wrote, with one consent, the German Bulthaupt and the Spanish Menendez y Pelayo, who, both of them, knew all the drama of the ages; "pain cannot groan or stammer, weep or wail". And by the present interpretation, I trust, the reader enjoys more of the spectator's liberty to appreciate this. The situation having been so boldly seized but deftly handled, the illusion so convincingly created and sustained, he is relieved of psychological questionings and realistic misgivings, and in mind and in heart can more unreservedly respond to the "simple, sensuous, and passionate" language of poetry and the stage. And (which to me is less, but not much less, important) by this interpretation he is not, in the end, out of harmony with what is (as I have indicated) essential in Coleridge's and De Quincey's appreciation of the play, that is, the dramatic disengaged from the psychological— in short, the situation—particularly as this appears in the words of the great disciple:

To me it is evident that Othello's state of feeling was not that of a degrading, suspicious rivalship, but the state of perfect misery, arising out of this dilemma, the most affecting, perhaps, to contemplate, of any which *can* exist—viz. the dire necessity of loving without limit one whom the heart pronounces to be unworthy of that love.[1]

---

[1] De Quincey's *Works* (Edin. 1863) XIV, 174.

Chapter III

PARALLELS, ANCIENT, MEDIEVAL, AND MODERN; IN THE DRAMA, THE EPIC, AND THE NOVEL

THE dramatic method which I have presented is, as I have indicated, not an anomaly, though in quality an indubitable exception. For other cases of the calumniator credited than those that have been or are to be mentioned, I must refer the reader to my monograph:[1] what now concerns me more is to show that this convention is not only not a fiction of my own, or an isolated phenomenon, peculiar to drama, but merely a particular form of a method, widespread and familiar, though by Shakespeare more skilfully employed than by any, of bringing about a daring and pregnant contrast, with a greater momentum to the story and a more unmingled sympathy for the hero, by an artificial or arbitrary intrusion or deception, human, magical, or divine. And what concerns me above all is to prove in this matter, not any indebtedness, but a kinship and natural solidarity in fiction; and to exhibit this constructive and concentrative, rather than mimetic and psychological, method in some of the greatest fiction in the world. For, as from the preceding chapter is apparent, it is my conviction that the clearest light attainable upon a piece of imaginative literature is that to be derived from

---

[1] *Othello*, especially pp. 5–9. It is to be found also in Corneille (*Mélite*), Lope (*El Acero de Madrid*), Tirso (*El Burlador*); and in story ancient or medieval it abounds, as in Apuleius and Boccaccio.

other such literature, whether or not of the same author-
ship, *genre*, period, or tongue.

§ 1

Cases in myth and legend, such as those of Abraham
and Isaac, Jephthah and his daughter, dramatic as they
are, we will pass by. In Euripides' *Hippolytus*, mentioned
above, there is not only the slander of the hero by
Phaedra, but the wrath of Aphrodite, bearing heavily,
though differently, upon them both, which, along with the
Nurse's artful and evil promptings, not only brings about
the complication but also in some part relieves the queen
of responsibility in our eyes. And in such fateful interventions the Greek tragedies and epics abound. There are
the notable ones of Orestes, Agamemnon at Aulis, and
Oedipus. Under obligation to avenge his father's death,
Orestes, who, in his moral bewilderment, consults the
oracle of Apollo, is bidden proceed, even against his
mother. He is nevertheless to be punished by the Furies
for so doing, but the situation is both ennobled and further
complicated through the god's command. In the *Iphigenia at Aulis*, indeed, all depends upon it; and the dictates
of piety and patriotism override those of a father's (and
also a husband's) love. And were it not for the oracle from
the fulfilment of which Oedipus fled, thus only to fulfil it,
and were it not for the curse upon his people, the cause of
which he pressed innocently but fearlessly forward to discover, the tragedy would not be one of the greatest in the
world. Here, as in the other tragedies mentioned, is the
improbable but most tragic of entanglements, the man's
nature being superior and contrary to his conduct, somewhat like that of Othello (and that of Hamlet, Lear, and

Macbeth, we shall see); though in the instance before us the unethical conduct is, save for the *hybris* of his inquiry, previous to the dramatic action. Here also, as in the case of three of the characters just mentioned, is the situation fairly (though not entirely) according to the ideal of Aristotle, of "a man not pre-eminently virtuous and just, whose misfortune, however, is brought upon him, not by vice or depravity, but by *some error of judgment*"; our pity, as he has just said, "being occasioned by undeserved misfortune, our fear by that of one like ourselves". Presently he reiterates the dictum, adding, "the man himself being either such as we have described, or better, not worse, than that".[1] And though there is no evidence that Shakespeare ever perused the Stagirite, or troubled himself (if he knew either) about Greek tragedy or comedy as a model (for he approached the unities only when adapting Plautus, or when, as in *Othello* and *The Tempest*, led to them by the nature of his material), he was, without knowing it, and simply by the consummation of his

---

[1] § 13. In my comparison of modern tragedy with the Greek I would not seem to be ignoring the distinctions pointed out by some great scholars. Ancient tragedy, at least in the hands of Aeschylus and Sophocles, was religious and moral; and concerned with the mystery, and if possible, the justification, of the ways of God. Motives not being so clearly distinguished as with us from deeds, the error of judgment is often equivalent to a fault; and ignorance is not, as with us, indulged. Moreover, the Aristotelian catharsis through pity and fear (or horror) belongs, in strictness, to ancient tragedy alone. But I have here to do, not with tragedy as a whole, but the situation; with the essential similarities in the matter of structure, of contrast and duplicity, not the differences; and I must not complicate my discussion by considering details, in themselves somewhat disputable. Professor Frye himself acknowledges (*Theory of Greek Tragedy*, Univ. Nebraska Studies, 1913, pp. 21–2) that the Aristotelian definition applies to all great tragedy in a general way.

development, at one with the Greeks in the central and pivotal conception. He was so far a Greek because he was the greatest, not of psychologists, but of dramatists.

In short, the method, arbitrary and artificial as it seems, is excellent; and it has been the making of the best tragedies (and epics too) in the world. It is a curious thing that the modern drama, which, in the interest of probability and psychology, presents the character as secreting its own poison, not inoculated with it, and as involved in the action, not in conflict with it, nevertheless does not much take to presenting this process directly upon the stage. The unities are observed, with the best of reasons. For in itself the process of psychical incubation is tardy and solitary, intangible and undramatic. Corneille and Racine, who initiated the modern method, observed the unities perforce; but Ibsen, under no classical constraint, did so deliberately, despite at this point the example of Shakespeare. And with all three the tragedy opens only as the air thickens and the storm threatens, while that humdrum pondering and dreary brooding—of Nora, the Alvings, the Rosmers, the Solnesses—which has been the cause of it, appears only in retrospect. Shakespeare's method of simplification and conventionalization, which we have been analysing, is really the best conceivable if, as with him, the whole story is presented on the stage; but it was also that of the ancients, who presented only the last act.

§ 2

Epics might seem to be beyond our purview; but Aristotle constantly cites Homer in speaking of tragedy, and once he says distinctly that the construction of an epic should be like that of a drama.[1] Anyone who has reflected on the matter will acknowledge that with the Greeks it is. As in tragedy and comedy both, the story begins in the middle of things; in so far as may be, the action is presented through the speech of the characters, not of the poet; and the long stretch of time covered is telescoped, in the *Iliad* to forty-seven days, in the *Odyssey* to forty-two. Even then narrative had decisively taken the direction which it still follows; and if all art constantly aspires towards the condition of music, all narrative art seems, more immediately, to aspire towards the condition of drama. What do we see nowadays but the novel itself, with Dostoyevsky and Conrad, James and Joyce, as well as the French, rather steadily becoming more dramatic, restricted in time and place and even (more dramatic than drama!) to one point of view?

Be that as it may, in the ancient and the medieval epics the *Othello* method, though without slander, is employed. Can Athena, as she stays the hand of Achilles when, in the opening scene of the *Iliad*, he is about to put an end to Agamemnon, be an allegory?[2] She is the goddess of wisdom, and here she may seem to be representing it. But to

---

[1] *Poetics*, 23.

[2] Since writing the above, I have happened upon Professor Bradley's interpretation of the episode (*Shakespearean Tragedy*, p. 348), which I had forgotten. It is in another connection, as a parallel to the relation between the Weïrd Sisters and Macbeth. The critic considers the goddess real and external, but as serving only to strengthen an inward movement in the mind of Achilles. Yet he is already drawing his great sword when she catches him by his golden hair; and Professor Bradley's interpretation seems to me to spoil the immediate as well as the subsequent situation, in both the epic and the tragedy. See below, pp. 87, 90. A boy's imagination is here a good test, and what boy would have Achilles here so tame? If by wisdom he be governed, it is of that pitiful sort which prefers abusive words to deeds!

the Greeks she was not the goddess of wisdom only but of war; and, at this early time, before all else a goddess. There is allegory in the *Iliad*, as when Strife or Discord appears upon the field; but it is of a simple and obvious sort. The fundamental objection to it here, however, is that it removes the obstacle, and relaxes the situation, not only at this juncture but in the whole long drama which ensues. If it be but wisdom that now stays the hand of the most fearless and fearful of the warriors, by thus keeping his character intact he really belies it, and makes meaningless or unheroic his bitter, abusive words as he acquiesces, as well as his wrathful sojourn subsequently in his tent. The whole dramatic value of that arises out of the eagerness for his participation, on the part of both the Greek army and Achilles himself—"yearning for the war-cry and for battle" (I, 492)—baffled by his pride. Only, therefore, as he bows to the deity, not the dictates of wisdom, are he and the army brought into that complication; and only as he is unavoidably thwarted in his purpose of retaliation at the outset is the reader's sympathy for a romantic hero, in a poem of warfare and derring-do, not of discretion and edification, caught and secured.

Also the other situations of the hero are, essentially, like that of Othello, and are treated in a similar way. As he chooses between long life, on the one hand, and fame, or (later) revenge for his friend, on the other, or between revenge for his friend and the promptings of humanity (and piety) as represented by the father of his foe, there is no analysis or hesitation, no inner debate or visible struggle. As with Othello—as with Antigone—that would have been to alienate some of the sympathy, trouble the situation, bedim the contrast. Again there is juxtaposition instead of alternation; but, though in the background, Achilles' feelings are perfectly apparent to the reader—his desire for life, his love for his friend, and his deep aversion to abating one jot or tittle of the full measure of the vindictive honours owing to him, at the end, just as is his yearning for battle after the quarrel at the beginning. In another essay than that cited at the close of Chapter II, in a different connection and without any reference to Othello, De Quincey perceives in this situation an equivalent artistic supremacy, which is partly due, as the writer seems to imply, to a similar construction:

Then we see him rise in his noontide wrath, before which no life could stand. The frenzy of his grief makes him for a time cruel and implacable. He sweeps the field of battle like a monsoon. His revenge descends perfect, sudden, like a curse from heaven....But the poet, before he would let him loose upon men, creates for him a sufficient, or at least palliating motive. In the sternest of his acts, we read only the anguish of his grief. This is surely the perfection of art.[1]

And if Aeneas, deserting Dido, were prompted by his own personal or nationalistic ambitions, not by a mandate from on high, what a sorry figure he would then be! Even as it is, he has lately been called "a brute",[2] though with the acknowledgment that he was not meant to be such; but how much more justified would have been the appellation if his conduct had been (as in the case of Othello, Macbeth, Lear, and Hamlet the critics would have it to be) quite in keeping with his character! Also Dido and Aeneas, Turnus and Amata act more speedily, and take more of our sympathy with them, as they fall in love because in-

---

[1] De Quincey's *Works* (Edin. 1863), v, 391.
[2] *Oxford Book of Latin Verse*, p. xix (H. W. Garrod).

flamed by Cupid at the instigation of Venus, or into a mad rage because inflamed by Allecto at the instigation of Juno. In the *Aeneid* and both the Homeric epics alike, the frequent divine promptings and interventions serve not only to relieve the character's responsibility but to preserve his prestige; as when a god or goddess snatches him up out of the combat (or "puts a weakling heart in his bosom"), deludes him or his enemy with a dream, misleads either by a wraith or by one person transformed into the likeness of another, or dazzles or beclouds his own or his enemy's eyes. In ancient epic are many of the constructional devices of deception later employed in Renaissance tragedy and comedy, though rarely those of a villain or a rogue.

Arnold, in the preface to the 1853 edition of his poems, observes that the best poems dealing with the details of modern life which pass daily under our eyes, leave the reader cold in comparison with the effect produced upon him by the latter books of the *Iliad*, by the Oresteia, or by the episode of Dido. "And why is this? Simply because in the three latter cases the action is greater, the personages nobler, the situations more intense; and this is the true basis of the interest in a poetical work, and this alone." The words apply equally to *Othello* as I have been endeavouring to present it; and the artifices of simplification and concentration adopted are much the same.

And what of the epical stories of the Middle Ages— Siegfried drinking his potion and forgetting Brünnhilde, and Tristram and Isolt drinking theirs and forgetting every one else in the world? Mr Robinson, in his *Tristram*, has put the potion aside; but, preserving realism, has lost a measure of the sympathy and dramatic effect. In the

63

older story knightly honour and the conjugal were not thus ignobly compromised; the sharp contrast between the lovers and their passion not thus broken or dulled.

§ 3

It is the same strategy, in epic and tragedy alike. It is that recommended by Dumas for drama nowadays—"l'audace, toujours l'audace". It is that recommended, more discreetly, by Dryden before him—"the boldest strokes of poetry, when they are managed artfully, are those which most delight the reader";[1] and the famous dramatist (and, justly, more famous critic) laments in his own masterpiece, *All for Love*, the lack of the very sort we have been discussing: "That which is wanting to work up the pity to a greater height was not afforded by the story; for the crimes of love, which they both committed, were not occasioned by any necessity,[2] or fatal ignorance, but were wholly voluntary". No more than the greatest is the Restoration playwright content with character its own fate, as in life—and criticism. He had rather be tragical than psychological, or ethical, or "true". In his tragedy he recognizes no doubt the defect that a subsequent neo-classicist and man of letters acknowledges, not merely in his own, but in that of his people in general, when Voltaire, who likewise knew both the ancients and Shakespeare, echoes Saint-Évremond as he declares that, in comparison, "nos pièces ne font pas une impression assez forte; que ce qui doit former la pitié fait tout au plus de la tendresse; que l'émotion tient lieu de saisissement, l'étonnement de l'horreur; qu'il manque à nos sentiments

[1] Apology prefixed to "The State of Innocence" (1677).
[2] *Necessitas*, of course.

quelque chose d'assez profond".[1] For in Corneille and
Racine psychology first comes into its own. But no
criticism so well fits and warrants the method of the Greeks
and Shakespeare, boldest and also subtlest of poets, as
that of the exquisite and penetrating Petronius Arbiter.
Not as in history, he says, "sed per ambages deorumque
ministeria...praecipitandus est liber spiritus, ut potius
furentis animi vaticinatio appareat quam religiosae
orationis sub testibus fides" (*Satyricon*, 119). Of which
Dryden remarks that "it is thought he taxes Lucan,...
[who] used not much the help of the heathen deities; there
was neither the ministry of the gods, nor the precipitation
of the soul, nor the fury of a prophet...in his *Pharsalia*;
he treats you more like a philosopher than a poet...in
one word, he walks soberly afoot, when he might fly".[2]
And Shakespeare?—He has both the wings and the will.

§ 4

Even in the placid and ample pages of the novel the
writer would walk not too soberly afoot, and calls in the
ministry of the gods. What else is that of the "heavy"
fathers, tyrannical guardians, or amorous and barbarous
aunts and duennas, in the eighteenth and nineteenth centuries, who thwart the course of others' love? Samuel
Butler, himself a novelist, goes so far astray as to take
Richardson and Fielding, Smollett and Jane Austen for
evidence that "at the beginning of the nineteenth century
the relations of parents and children were still far from
satisfactory"; and the drama, no doubt, for evidence,
when he makes out such relations in Elizabethan times to

[1] *Appel à toutes les Nations, Œuvres* (1879), XXIV, 218.
[2] *Of Heroic Plays* (1672).

have been on the whole more kindly. Things got worse, it seems—if novels be social documents.[1] The difference is really in the art—between a scene public and patrician, on the one hand, and one domestic and bourgeois, on the other. The heavy father (though there he too sometimes appears) is like Fate or the Sovereign, the villain or the rival, in Elizabethan and Restoration drama. In the novel itself the villain lingers on till after Dickens and Thackeray; as well as the other means or methods of deception—disguise and mistaken identity, eavesdropping and letter-reading—a beautiful woman as a man playing a big part so late as in Gautier's *Mademoiselle de Maupin*. To be sure, the situation thus produced is rather external: in English novels, at least, the hero or heroine is not often a prey to two passions side by side, like Othello; or pitted against each other, like Phèdre or Hermione. Nevertheless, there is here, for a similar structural purpose, an irrational element, such as we have been finding, to be allowed for. The fond parents of the delightful young people are suddenly outrageous, leaving no stone unturned—no door unlocked or hard word unuttered—to wreck their lifelong happiness. And the daughters seem strangely patient and dutiful; or, considering the treatment they receive, strangely affectionate and attached; but, they and their lovers alike, woefully lacking in cleverness or enterprise. Seldom in novels till these latter days, and not often then, are the lets and hindrances limited to those which naturally but slowly and undemonstratively arise in the hearts or out of the circumstances of the young people themselves; seldom do the

[1] Cf. my *Shakespeare Studies* (1927), Chap. ii, and an article in the *Pub. Mod. Lang. Assoc.* March, 1932, entitled "Literature and Life Again".

situations lie merely in the contrasts and conflicts, ironies and paradoxes, of character or sex.

In the above paragraph I have, as is apparent, been glancing at *Tom Jones*, which at one point I have already cited as an example of naturalness in response to gossip. Sophia is rather exceptional. Allworthy, though an intelligent and kindly man, genuinely attached to Tom, seems to have as little real acquaintance with him, and with Blifil and Thwackum (who complain of him and slander him), despite years of living with them all, as, with far less opportunity, has Othello with Desdemona, Cassio, and Iago. Near the end of the big book we are told that he had never loved or esteemed Thwackum, and (which is improbable in itself) had retained his services as tutor only for his scholarship and assiduity: why, then, at so fateful a juncture should the Squire have taken his word? He pursues no careful inquiry, holds no judicial hearing, and sees no necessity of rousing Tom out of his grief and despair to speak up for himself. By Blifil, on the other hand, he is hoodwinked, along with Western and his sister, from the beginning; like Othello, he cannot see anything until the last situation of the last act, and then sees all at once. Thereupon Tom is taken again to his bosom; and with still less of a chance to defend himself, Blifil, as a "viper", is cast out of it. The one process corresponds to the other—what has been done is now undone—but neither corresponds to normal human nature and conduct. So lightly one cannot pass from belief and affection to disbelief and hatred, and back again. The human mind is not so immediately receptive and responsive: it resists and reacts, and (if the inner motive be strong enough) even against what to others would be the

5-2

most unimpeachable testimony and the most convincing evidence. And this no one knows better than Fielding himself, when the plot or a situation is not at stake. Yet in the service of these he employs also most of the other arbitrary and artificial devices which we have mentioned; and it is partly by his skill in handling them, and his power in presenting character by means of them (or in spite of them) that he attained to fame. However, his book is not a drama or a poem; and the devices are not made to serve a necessary function of the dramatic economy, or the higher one of a unifying illusion.

Clarissa, in which they are employed as abundantly, but somewhat less frankly, is a better parallel. Here is another improbable situation—a whole family, hitherto to the clever and charming heroine devoted, suddenly bent on making her for ever wretched as the wife of a man she properly despises, in order, simply because of her brother's quarrel, to keep her from Lovelace, whose advances they have previously welcomed and she has no open thought of encouraging herself; and on driving her, by their persecutions, torments, and menaces, despite every justifiable concession on her part, into his power. It is the last thing that, in the flesh, this pink of propriety would have done; or that her relatives, if they loved her, and were in their senses, would have driven her to do. "Good God of Heaven and Earth!" cries Miss Howe, her confidante, at the news, long before the dire, irremediable consequences. "The step you have been forced upon on one hand", she says again, "and tricked into on the other! A strange fatality!"[1] *Ambages deorumque ministeria!* And what the novelist is seeking is the further situation of a noble and

[1] IV, letter 16.

innocent woman seduced by a haughty and resentful, intriguing and sadistic Don Juan, like that of Othello in the clutches of Iago (and like that of Desdemona—at the same time loved and tortured—in his own), together with the startling contrast and relief of such unlikely company, though at the cost of even a lesser measure of fault in the victim; and the tragic irony and paradox, the balance or reconcilement of opposite or discordant qualities, are continually impressed upon us. "Flying from friends she was resolved not to abandon, to the man she was determined not to go off with.... How could I be such a villain to so divine a creature? Yet love her all the time, as never man loved woman!"[1]

But the price to pay—the improbabilities, as real as in the tragedy—is, as in a novel it may be, better concealed. The dubious period, frequently alluded to, when the family were fond of the daughter, and were reasonable enough for her to have been fond of them, and the house was the home of peace and quiet, is previous to the narrative; and the stratagems and contrivances of Lovelace within and without the household, the means whereby Clarissa, under restraint, keeps in correspondence with him and others, as well as her motives in his case for beginning it,[2] together with the scruples against fleeing with Miss Howe or to Lady Betty's instead, are generally kept in the background, or slurred over, or in some way, however unsatisfactory, explained. What is perhaps the greatest improbability— that Lovelace should love one so virtuous, and still

---

[1] III, letter 5; VIII, letter 18.
[2] The motive which she recognizes is the specious one of allaying his resentment; but in retrospect she realizes the truth of Miss Howe's opinion that she was more interested in him than she was aware.

pursue her and seek to marry her after he has ruined her, and when she hates and detests him—is, "for the moment", made acceptable by the (less obviously improbable) breadth of the conception—his Satanic pride and ambition, his erotic cruelty and curiosity, and his aesthetic taste. "For there is beauty in everything she says and does! Beauty in her passion! Beauty in her tears!"[1] And the improbability of her thinking of marrying him when she already half knows him, or of her best friend's urging it upon her after they both know him altogether, is made tolerable by the widespread and time-honoured fallacies of the possibility of reform and of marriage as man's proper amends to woman.

In the foreground, moreover, there is probability enough. As in Shakespeare, there is, from the prosaic point of view, half-truth; from the artistic, what no doubt Mr Aldous Huxley would call "super-truth"; and the latter, by virtue, not of the story or (in the last analysis) of the psychology, but of the plastic, differentiating power over trait and speech. I wonder if in any other novel, in any language, people are so perfectly distinguished by what they say or write. Whether psychology play a part at all depends on the word as we define it; and even if so, it would be within limits, however large—those of the situation and the author's purpose. To the villain-hero the words of Professor Phelps apply, as (if he permit) they may also to the central characters of Shakespeare's plays, Iago and Othello, Hamlet, Lear, and Macbeth: "Analyse him—he simply will not do; no such person ever lived".[2] But, like them, Lovelace is not meant for a

[1] v, letter 21.
[2] Novels of Richardson (1902), v, xxx. Cf. for Iago, my *Shakespeare Studies*, pp. 382–91.

person merely; he is here too big and there too little, because, at either point, too much a part of the situation. He is part of a novel, they are parts of plays. And to the contradiction in the heroine there is a double aspect, corresponding to the author's dual purpose. The priggish old printer, on the one hand, was undertaking, at the same time, to teach fathers and daughters a lesson and to show them a pattern. The imaginative genius, on the other hand, like the Elizabethan and the Hellenic without knowing it, was striving for what is in many ways the most tragic plight, and certainly the most poignant—a character, like Othello's, meeting a destiny of which it has *not* had the making—a spirit unfortunate, but *not*

> betray'd by what is false within,—

"a penitent without a fault", as the rake Belford says of her, and arousing a sympathy that is well-nigh without alloy. And to heighten this emotional effect, at the expense of the psychology, the heroine is, like Othello and Hamlet, Lear and (in part) Macbeth, made the object of almost universal admiration and lamentation (though here overdone), even, amid their resentment, on the part of the family and also of the Don Juan himself.

In later novels, also, where psychology plays an acknowledged and increasingly important part, is to be found, in various forms, such a contrived and improbable contrast, but surcharged situation, such a product of simplification and intensification as we have been exhibiting. To this day, for the sake of its compactness and brevity, and despite the demand for originality, it lingers on, more or less modified and disguised, in the short story; and we still have deception and feigning, eavesdropping and twins that are mistaken, ghosts, trances, and dreams. For more

71

than a century, however, in story, novel, and drama alike, it has, frequently, been replaced by the contrast that may, actually or apparently, be discovered among primitives (such as Corsicans or Hindoos, criminals, social outcasts or rebels); or among special trades or professions, whether in opposition to the standard morality of Europe, or within themselves as they cultivate *one* virtue at the expense of others—though shedding blood not thieving, though thieving and lying not fornicating, though robbing strangers not betraying a comrade, though wicked devout, and making of their virtue, their vice or trade, a point of honour. More recently, for a similar purpose, as well as the inherent interest, psychological abnormalities and sexual perversions have been employed. But as late as 1886, in Hardy's *Mayor of Casterbridge*, a fairly long novel and a great one, something of the artificial and arbitrary contrast reappears, though rather of the sort in *King Lear* than in the tragedy we have been discussing. Near the beginning Henchard, under the stress of poverty and the influence of drink, sells his wife and child; and thenceforward, and forthwith, the author has the advantage of a hero apparently single and really married, not unlike that of Shakespeare's wise and loving father who has been foolish and cruel, his unsuspicious husband who is jealous, and (as we are yet to see) his brave and honourable warrior who is a traitor and assassin. And as the past recoils upon the present there are Elizabethan complications and ironies. But a better parallel is with the medieval epics. Drink and drugs, still turned to account in the novel and the short story, that a man may do what by nature he would not, are not unlike the magic potions.

In Thackeray, in the fifties, there is, several times, the

same contrivance as in *Othello*—the suspicion of the loved one by the pure-minded and innocent; but by women, not men, and without the villain to suggest it, the consistent illusion, or the dramatic or poetic method or effect: Helen and Laura, who believe Pendennis has fallen into Fanny's toils; the Lambert ladies, who think the like of Henry Warrington in connection with the Cattarina; and Madam Warrington and her friends, in Virginia, who, having welcomed George (newly returned from captivity) as from the grave, turn against him on the Indian girl's appearing to claim the ransom. In the first two instances, at least, there is nothing in the women to warrant such thoughts, neither a suspicious (or jealous) nature nor a previous disillusioning experience. And, in default of a treatment like Shakespeare's, there is nothing to lend them credibility but what psychology is involved in the narrative device of slander—the sophism that trustfulness leads to distrust, innocence to suspicion; and what of it is involved in not only this but other narrative devices of deception—the presumption that old acquaintances have no knowledge of each other's characters, even as (in the case of disguise) of their persons. This psychology does not content us. Shakespeare, of course, like the ancients before him, knew that in such a matter, in such circumstances, one is not so dependent upon hearsay, or so inclined to listen; and Thackeray, of course, knew that one is not so dependent even upon what the friend says himself. For a purpose—an effect, and in this latter instance, a poor one—they wrote plays or novels as if they knew it not. But now that this artificial construction is out of favour, human character has, in the best novels and plays, regained some of its natural transparency; and in James, for instance, there

73

is often, as in life, a process of "mute communication", whether intentional or unintentional; people coming, like Maria Gostrey in the opera-box, to just conclusions regarding others without report or inquiry, even without interrogation or discussion.

This is a different art, whether in the novel, the drama, or the epic, from that of Thackeray or Fielding, Shakespeare or Homer, and more nearly approaches reality. In the novel, where contrasts and striking situations are not so indispensable, they must be more plausible—like the contrast in Mann's *Zauberberg*, between the life in the hospital and that outside—though, for the most part, they are those of character, point of view, and the sex relation, and (without deliberate deception) between reality and appearances, and between possession and desire. Maupassant, who was a realist if ever there was one, sees and presents the purpose and method of this art clearly:

Le romancier, au contraire, qui prétend nous donner une image exacte de la vie, doit éviter avec soin tout enchaînement d'événements qui paraîtrait exceptionnel. Son but n'est point de nous raconter une histoire, de nous amuser ou de nous attendrir, mais de nous forcer à penser, à comprendre le sens profond et caché des événements....

Au lieu de machiner une aventure et de la dérouler de façon à la rendre intéressante jusqu'au dénouement, il prendra son ou ses personnages à une certaine période de leur existence et les conduira, par des transitions naturelles, jusqu'à la période suivante....

L'habileté de son plan ne consistera donc point dans l'émotion ou dans le charme, dans un début attachant ou dans une catastrophe émouvante, mais dans le groupement adroit de petits faits constants d'où se dégagera le sens définitif de l'œuvre...il devra savoir éliminer, parmi les menus événements innombrables et quotidiens, tous ceux qui lui sont inutiles, et mettre en lumière, d'une façon spéciale, tous ceux qui seraient démeurés inaperçus pour des observateurs peu clairvoyants et qui donnent au livre sa portée, sa valeur d'ensemble...tous les fils si minces, si secrets, presque invisibles...à la place de la ficelle unique qui avait nom: l'Intrigue.   Preface to *Pierre et Jean* (1909), pp. xi, xii.

That is to say, the structure is less clear-cut and more elusive, less boldly coloured and more plausibly motivated, yet is the product of a simplification and compression none the less. Shakespeare, as we have seen already, has decidedly more than the single thread; but as Maupassant says, in the modern novel (less consistently, perforce, in the drama) it is no longer a matter of a striking story or situation, an attractive beginning or moving catastrophe, but of the skilful massing and arrangement, with natural transitions, of numerous traits and facts, which shall, not entertain or arouse us, but force us to think. Such words, even the last, are not equally appropriate to the writers above named. They, also, force us to think, but still more to see and feel. And yet this of Maupassant's, too, is but art—is only on the page. Character or incident, as with those greater writers, is *not* a slice of life:

Le réaliste, s'il est un artiste, cherchera, non pas à nous montrer la photographie banale de la vie, mais à nous en donner la vision plus complète, plus saisissante, plus probante que la réalité même....
La vie encore laisse tout au même plan, précipite les faits ou les traîne indéfiniment. L'art, au contraire, consiste à user des précautions et des préparations, à ménager des transitions savantes et dissimulées, à mettre en pleine lumière,

par la seule adresse de la composition, les événements essentiels et à donner à tous les autres le degré de relief qui leur convient, suivant leur importance, pour produire la sensation profonde de la vérité spéciale qu'on veut montrer.

Faire vrai consiste donc à donner l'illusion complète du vrai, suivant la logique ordinaire des faits, et non à les transcrire servilement dans le pêle-mêle de leur succession.

J'en conclus que les Réalistes de talent devraient s'appeler plutôt des Illusionistes. Pp. xiv, xv.

And the critics who have treated Shakespeare's creatures as if they were psychological specimens to analyse or documents to decipher seem for the time to have forgotten the nature even of the literary art of their own day.

Chapter IV

MACBETH

§ 1

I MUST now move more rapidly (save in the case of *Hamlet*, to be sure), confining myself, for the most part, to a general indication of a similar method in the other chief tragedies. It is followed in both *Hamlet* and *Macbeth*; as I had pointed out before reading Mr Robert Bridges' essay on *The Influence of the Audience in Shakespeare*, though to it and Mr Middleton Murry's seal of approval put upon it[1] I am greatly indebted, not only for confirming but for clarifying my views.[2] In the latter play (on which Mr Bridges centred his attention) is the same contradiction or antinomy—a brave and honourable man plunged into cowardly and dishonourable conduct; an ambitious man with his thoughts, both before and after the crime, set, not upon the reasons which would impel or justify him, but upon those which would deter him. Still more noticeably than in *Othello*,[3] the dramatist has deliberately passed over the motives or justifications—Macbeth's grievances against Duncan, the king's feeble government and his general's stronger and juster one in the sequel—furnished him in

[1] *The New Adelphi*, Dec. 1927, pp. 159–60.

[2] It is necessary to speak thus exactly, for to some scholars I may seem in my monographs to have profited by the Poet Laureate's views without acknowledgment. Buried in the great Shakespeare Head edition (1907), his essay met my eye only after *Hamlet* (1919).

[3] Cf. below, p. 97, for Iago; above, p. 12, for Othello himself.

the source. The contrast, again, the emotional effect, was what he was seeking. "The interest in the tragedy of *Macbeth*", says Mr Bridges, "is the perpetration of a crime by a man whose magnificent qualities of mind, extreme courage, and poetic imagination, raise the villainies above common meanness and give occasion for a superhuman conflict of images and ideas".[1] "The terror the tragedy inspires", says Mr J. J. Chapman, "is due to the abyss that lies between the inner natures of Macbeth and Lady Macbeth, and the murder which they perpetrate".[2] And that, according to what we have ordinarily been taught, is neither psychology nor tragedy.

How, then, does Macbeth, checked by his conscience, ever come to the point, or seem to us to do so? Like Othello, he is made real and convincing by his tone and accent, apart from his conduct; and, despite his horror, he is impelled by supernatural promptings and his wife's persuasions, as, despite his love, Othello is impelled by the conviction forced upon him by Iago's arts. What "predisposition" there is within him, "if it be allowed to be only in the exact balance required for these other agencies to carry it, is still contradictory to the picture of nobility impressed on us by Shakespeare, and essential to his drama".[3] Here, again, is an un-psychological contrast or conflict; and the apparent incentive is external. In neither of the heroes do motives—of ambition or of jealousy— shine through thought or deed; in neither of them do such motives meet in a real clash or prolonged contention with

---

[1] Bridges, *op. cit.* p. 327.

[2] *A Glance toward Shakespeare* (1922), p. 71. Mr Chapman does not pursue the subject. Cf. opinions of others to the same effect, my *Shakespeare Studies*, p. 91.   [3] Bridges, *op. cit.* p. 327.

the man's nobler nature. That is the way, as we have seen, in French drama, not in the Shakespearean or the Greek. As neither Antigone, nor Oedipus, nor Orestes ever hesitates or vacillates, so really does not Othello or Macbeth. And in the latter, as in the former, there is a tragic development, by way, not of the hero's inner struggle, his turning from this resolve to that, but of his fairly continual fall (marked by the stages of a story, not of an inner debate) as from shelf to shelf down the precipice.

For both dramatist and audience had not the modern psychological interest and bias. To them no doubt Othello's belief in the representations of one so repeatedly called honest seemed no more than did disguise, or the playing of a part, as by Hamlet, or the substitution of one woman for another at a rendezvous, as in *All's Well* and *Measure for Measure*, or in matrimony, as (near the end) in *Much Ado*, to be quite the barefaced artifice that it would seem to-day. And the conscience in both Macbeth and his Lady, which so fearfully torments him beforehand and both of them afterwards, for what he in part and she nearly altogether desired to do, was, in keeping with the theological conception of it, prevalent then and even now familiar, not so much the assertion of a righteous nature within the individual himself, as the voice of his creator, or "fire let down from Heaven", or the worm that never dies. It was Nemesis, casting its shadow before, rather than repentance.

These two circumstances—the traditional indifference to psychological analysis and the traditional conception of the conscience—made it possible (or necessary) for Shakespeare and other Elizabethan dramatists, confronting such material, to adopt a simplification, or short-cut, particularly welcome in a tragedy which covers the whole story, with numerous characters and incidents, not merely, as does the French, the last stage or stretch of it. Not presented, the conflict is suggested. The deterrents directly and plainly appear; and the strength of the hero's incentives or desires may be inferred from his conduct, even from his horror of it, and from the fatal and the conjugal promptings to which he yields. In French tragedy the hero gives utterance to his desires and incentives, leaving to his beloved or his confidant the counsels of honour or duty; or else the hero considers alternately both sides of the question himself: and all in an emotional debate, with a fluctuating movement, which takes up the larger part of the play. Thus we see clearly, as not in *Macbeth*, how he comes to act and why; but action is for long in abeyance. In *Macbeth* the process is swifter and more summary. Parts of four short scenes—less than two hundred lines—suffice for it. And it is much the same method, at about the same time, as in Heywood's *Woman Killed with Kindness*, though there both temptation and fall take place within the limits of a single scene.[1] Still more than Macbeth, both Wendoll and Mrs Frankford speak against the tenor of what they are doing, and (save in the mere fact of their doing it) their inclination appears chiefly in the guise of Destiny, against which they exclaim. To one accustomed to the French method, intent upon psychology, all three characters may seem irrational, sinning against their will. But the contrast, in both plays, is made clear enough: only the conflict is intimated or implied. The battle we do not witness, in its changes, but hear it from afar.

[1] Act II, sc. iii.

Here are the makings of drama, no question—and the
psychology lacking has, by the critics, been duly supplied.
But, like that provided for Othello, it is unreal and specious; yet, like it, again, when reduced to its lowest terms,
almost equivalent to the purely dramatic and poetic explanation that I offer.[1] The critics' perceptions are right,
only their interpretations are wrong. "The deed is done
in horror", says Mr Bradley, "and without the faintest
desire or sense of glory—done, one may almost say, as if
it were an appalling duty"—which, though true, is not
psychology, but really amounts to what I have said
above. It is no more psychology than Bradley's and
Raleigh's and the others' explanation of Othello—"His
trust where he trusts is absolute"[2]—which, when we stop
to think of it, makes him worse than a Potiphar or
Proetus! *They* hearkened not unto strangers but unto
their wives. It is a good thing in criticism, if not always in
poetry and drama, to call things by their proper names.
"Trust", "horror", "duty"—"when I make a word do a
lot of work like that", says Humpty Dumpty, "I always
pay it extra". The only psychology possible for Macbeth
is a morbid or abnormal sort, which would have him
tempted as by the sight of cold steel to plunge it into you,
or as by an abyss to jump into it; but that, not clearly
indicated, is out of the question for a popular tragic hero
in the time of Elizabeth; or (to speak historically) a great
general and champion in the time of Edward the Con-
fessor, when Scottish Earls were still thanes, and the law
of succession was not yet fixed, who, after in his own castle
both the king and his supposed murderers have been
murdered, proceeds, unchallenged, with a primitive facility

---

[1] See above, p. 17.   [2] *Shakespearean Tragedy* (1903), p. 191.

and promptitude, to Scone to be invested. That Shakespeare would have no psychology of any sort to obscure his contrast, is made clear by his depriving the hero of his historical and natural motives, and piling on the head of the simple regicide in Holinshed crimes against the primal laws of hospitality and humanity, so as almost to rob him of the very name of hero and turn him into a villain instead.

How shall that sorry outcome be avoided? The dramatist has here undertaken something more audacious and perilous than even in *Othello*. He has widened the cleft between character and conduct; in that this brave and honourable man, with no grievance, and with his thoughts bent upon the heinousness of the crime, and little on the sweet fruition of an earthly crown, kills, asleep, an old man, his guest and his king, who has borne himself so clear in his high office, loved and trusted him, and showered honours on him. By the nature of the case the burden of this responsibility cannot, as with Othello, be laid upon the shoulders of the instigators—the Weird Sisters and his wife—for thus the dignity of the hero would be too much lowered in our eyes. They may only urge him on; but Iago deludes Othello, who—and this in drama is important—acts of himself. And by the nature of the case the hero cannot be made so noble and sympathetic as Othello at the outset—for thus his subsequent conduct would in the circumstances be revolting. Since he is not labouring under a strong delusion, he must from the deed be not wholly averse.

§ 2

How, then, is the hero to be kept from playing the villain's rôle, in defiance of Aristotle, of drama? There is manœuvring, and more of it than in *Othello*. The murder, for one thing, is not committed on the stage, though in Elizabethan tragedy it nearly always is. Macbeth, with so little reason, cannot be permitted to kill before our eyes an old man, his sovereign, his guest, his greatest benefactor, as can Othello, under the compulsion of the "strong conception that he does groan withal", his beloved wife; and we are witnesses of the high crime only by way of the murderers' broken and horror-stricken remembrance. And, for another thing, that cool colloquy on regicide, previous to the prophecy, between the hero and the heroine, to which she once refers—"Nor time nor place did then adhere"—is not presented either; "plainly", Mr Bridges observes, "such a scene would destroy the drama". Indeed, if we are to judge from the text, "the poet does not wish us to be clearly determined whether Macbeth had planned the murder beforehand, or had been led by supernatural soliciting, or was mainly urged by his wife".[1] There is a "veiled confusion of motive"; or the motives seem, though still in uncertainty, to conspire:

"Shakespeare...makes Lady Macbeth", says Mr Bridges, "represent the advent of Duncan to their castle as a favourable opportunity; and he knows that the audience, blinded by the material juxtaposition, will regard it as such. But to propose this dastardly violation of honour to Macbeth would, most probably, have stimulated his nobility, and scared him from the crime however fully he might have been predetermined on it: yet Shakespeare, fortifying the position by Lady Mac-

[1] Bridges, *op. cit.* p. 329.

6-2

beth's ambition and will, ventures to exhibit his hero as truly possessed by the proper shame and horror, but fascinated by the presentation which is deluding the audience".[1]

The spectral dagger tempts him—Fate lures him on; but hedging and finesse are not enough. In large measure the poet's success in overcoming the objectionable effects of the big and bold situation which he has created, is owing, as both the Poet Laureate and Professor Frye have noticed, to the power and skill with which the character is enforced upon the audience: "for it is when their minds are preoccupied with his personality that the actions follow as unquestionable realities, and in the *Macbeth* even pre-ordained and prophesied".[2] In all these various ways, then, their reason, their logical and natural expectations, are not frankly and directly satisfied, but circumvented or overridden.

In the incidents there is less of unquestionable reality than in the characters, one and all; these in Shakespeare generally are not, as in Racine and Ibsen, coextensive with their conduct, or always in harmony with it, but are presented also from other sides and convince in their own right. They are presented in the round, and start up from the canvas. They utter thoughts and sentiments not strictly required for the business in hand, and appear also in simple and humble relations. In Macbeth and his wife, indeed, this is less noticeable than in Othello, Hamlet, and Lear, Brutus, Romeo, and Coriolanus; but perhaps still more than any of these they are vivified and transfigured by the power of poetry.

This works not so much upon them as within them, and particularly through the conscience; by that more than

[1] *Ibid.* pp. 329–30.   [2] *Ibid.* p. 329.

by any charm or native nobility of character, such as is
in the other heroes apparent, the sympathies of the
audience are touched and retained. Not so much repentance as retribution, it nevertheless speaks, in the thane
and his lady, by his or her own individual voice, out of his
or her own experience; and they are ennobled by the
utterance of such thoughts and feelings, however (in the
last analysis) inappropriate, and by their moral sufferings,
however improbable. "[The expressions]", says Maeterlinck, "are continually borrowed from the environment
of the characters, and, by preference, from the noblest, the
hugest things of heaven and earth, in such a way that the
men themselves form the atmosphere which they breathe
and, at the same time, become the tragic creatures of the
atmosphere which they create."[1] In modern times the
professional psychologists, who, if not with poetic taste,
are blest with candour, have, unaware of this traditional,
external nature of the conscience, taken Macbeth, as
warned by it so clearly and vividly before the deed, and
moved to lamentation so immediately thereupon, for a
coward, hypocrite, or sentimentalist, or all three of these
together. "Mere poetical whining", they cry, "over his
most merited situation!" For they suppose him to be ambitious and ruthless by nature, not, mainly, by a conjunc-
tion of influences and circumstances. But is it not just so
that some of the critics have taken Othello to be either
suspicious or stupid; and Lear, of late, to be habitually
irascible and tyrannical;[2] which is, to use the phrase of

[1] *Fortnightly Review*, XCIII, 699.

[2] Cf. Miss L. B. Campbell's *Shakespeare's Tragic Heroes* (1930); Dover
Wilson's *Essential Shakespeare*, pp. 125–7. And see below, p. 138. I have
dealt with this learned but (as I think) unsympathetic criticism in an un-
published article entitled "Literature and Life Once More".

demonstration, "contrary to the hypothesis", and contrary still more to tragedy? A predisposition in the character is the postulate of their thought. Maeterlinck, a modern poet and dramatist, instinctively reads the text aright, with evidently more than an inkling of such a conception of dramatic condensation and contrast as we have been presuming. "Nowhere shall we discover three acts of which the tragic situation is so dense, so gloomily abundant, so naturally profound, where, while remaining so simple, so conventional, in appearance, it is nevertheless of a poetic quality so high, so intense, so precious. Nowhere shall we behold a group of human beings, with its own atmosphere, that prolongs its terrifying and secret existence in the words, both in the book and on the stage, in the manner of this group".[1]

Indeed, as in *Othello* and all other Shakespearean tragedy, it is in large measure this power of poetry that vivifies, "credibilizes", and even propels the play. It is this that makes us feel the force of conscience in the hero, and of the ambition, in him and his Lady, which overrides it; of the Fate which instigates the murderers, and of their horror both before and after the deed. We at once see the difference as we turn to *Mourning Becomes Electra*, with its dead prose and its undifferentiated style, its psychology and (with due allowances for "expressionism") its naked and ugly reality, and then recall its lofty and distant model, in Aeschylus. Not in O'Neill's play but in *Macbeth*, and in the *Agamemnon*, do we find the thing itself—in its whole tremendous import and impact—the higher reality, the super-truth. Not in O'Neill's play do we find, with a sufficient passion before and after—with ample tragic

[1] *Fortnightly Review*, XCIII, 695.

warrant and emphasis at any time—what we cannot but acknowledge to be murder.

§ 3

Also, as in *Othello*, the dramatist is concerned for the establishing and preserving of the illusion by a musical treatment, particularly in the matter of a fatal influence, an ironical retaliation. In no other of Shakespeare's tragedies is the supernatural so prominent or so potent; for the Weird Sisters are no more subjective or symbolical than is Athena in the *Iliad*, or the Eumenides in Aeschylus, otherwise (as there) the situation would be ruined.[1] They play both the rôles—temptation and retribution—as do the devils in the Christian system; Nature itself, here no mere background, being in league with them. The immediate fulfilment of their prophecy that Glamis shall be Cawdor, commented upon by the three who know of it, lends credibility to the other prophecies which ensue. And not once nor twice only do the Sisters put in an appearance: the spell that they weave with their solemn, uncanny ritual reaches even beyond the fourth act, as by the various reiteration of the phrases about Birnam Wood coming to Dunsinane, and about fearing no man of woman born, are developed all the possibilities of irony. There are irony and nemesis, both, in the murdered warrior's appearing at the feast to which he had been invited, as a ghost; and in the vision of the line of kings, headed by Malcolm and terminated by the descendants of

---

[1] Cf. above, p. 60. Obviously, if the Sisters *signify*, or symbolize, "temptation and retribution", they no longer lighten the load of responsibility upon the hero. But the primary consideration is that such a meaning is un-Shakespearean. Cf. my *Shakespeare Studies*, chap. v, "The Ghosts".

Banquo, "who smiles upon me and points at them for
his". And Nature? Night is invoked before the first
murder by the heroine and before the next by the hero,
and it wraps them round. The "spirits that tend on
mortal thoughts", they come but do not go. There is
fatal fascination in the vision of the dagger, and retribution in the voice that cries, "Sleep no more". Sleep, where
Night holds sway, with its laughter and misgivings, sighs
and remorseful mutterings, and terrible dreams, plays a
big and repeated part in the story. And the raven himself
is hoarse that croaks the fatal entrance; the owl shrieks,
the fatal bellman; the horses of Duncan, it is reported, eat
each other; there is a storm, and even afar, where Lennox
lay, there have been lamentings heard in the air, strange
screams of death, and accents terrible. Like the tempest
in *King Lear* and that attended with supernatural por-
tents in *Julius Caesar*, this demonstration is (again) not
a modern symbol, not a poetic echo of either men's passions or their deeds, but a means of emotional emphasis
which derives authority from a superstitious notion, not
then extinct, that the fall or murder of monarchs was
portended or accompanied by an upheaval in Nature,
whether in sympathy or in revulsion. This ambiguity or
contradiction, as in the function, noted above, of the
Weird Sisters, of Night and the deadly spirits that attend
her, and even somewhat as in the "veiled confusion ·of
motive" at the outset, but serves the dramatic purpose.
Hero and heroine seem tangled in a net, partly of their
weaving. These sinister utterances and dispositions, moreover, waken echoes within. The demonic conscience of the
two murderers is itself, as we have seen, a nemesis; and
one of its chief means of torment is to summon up re-

membrance of things past. The Lady, in her sleep-walking, still hears the knocking at the gate, which had continued, with drunken mimicry and unconsciously apposite comment, till the Porter opened it; and, thus musically treated, almost as if of retribution a symbol, it fairly reverberates through the play. Now in such a potency of Fate, such a malignity of Nature, Shakespeare probably no more believed than in that of the villain; yet he believes in it, and leads us to do likewise, "for the moment", within the magic circle he has drawn. On the belief the tragedy, in its poetic purposes, depends.

Chapter V

HAMLET

§ 1

In *Hamlet*, also, though in a different manner, the hero is put in a plight—made superior to his conduct and somewhat averse to it. Again the highly effective situation is brought about by external means—by the ghost, which is, of course, no figment of the hero's imagination, and no more an allegory or symbol than is the goddess Athena in the epic or the Weird Sisters in the tragedy, who perform much the same dramatic function. And again the improbabilities are allayed by the reality of the characterization, the interest of a quickly moving story, a veiled confusion of motive, and the all-reconciling power of poetry.

Of the dramatist's particular purpose, however, and his success in achieving it, we are here less able rightly to judge because the original *Hamlet* is lost; though of this we indirectly know enough (that is, through the sister play *The Spanish Tragedy*, by the same author; the German *Hamlet*; and Quarto I, which is Shakespeare's first revision, piratically printed and inadequately reported)[1]

---

[1] The dates of *The Spanish Tragedy* and the old *Hamlet* are prior to 1589; and the old *Hamlet* is probably previous to the other play for the simple reason that the story of the latter is the Belleforest Hamlet story transposed, a father revenging instead of the son. That Kyd was the author of the old *Hamlet* is as certain as any attribution founded on indirect evidence can be. The First Quarto was published in 1603; *Der Bestrafte Brudermord* is in a MS. of 1710, though it must have been written much earlier, and is based either on Kyd direct or Quarto I. Marston's *Antonio's Revenge* (c. 1599–1600), being, like his other tragedies, under Kyd's influence, repeats *Hamlet* situations and follows its technique.

to be sure that for the resulting obscurity it was much to blame. This rudely written but cunningly constructed Senecan melodrama of Kyd's was popular—hence the two revisions of it by the most popular dramatist of the London stage; and yielding to the demand of his company and their public, the poet was not free, if indeed, in view of the practical necessities and advantages, he was much disposed, to make sweeping changes. Until his life-giving hand retouched it the play had not been so popular as *The Spanish Tragedy*, which had, in the last months, taken a new lease of life from the mad-scenes added by Jonson; it was this success that the Chamberlain's company was now emulating; and since the most unreasonable features of the Danish tragedy, shared by the Spanish, were its most unmistakable attractions, they must be not only retained but, in Jonson's fashion, heightened and set off. The story must in general be the same story, though better told, or both company and public would be disappointed; and the principal improvement expected was no doubt in style and metre.

With merely that Shakespeare could not have contented himself, but just how far was he to go? Because not only of the popular demand but of dramatic requirements, the ghost must still appear at the beginning, and the tragic deed be accomplished, as in all good revenge plays, ancient or modern, at the end. How, then, was the revenger to be occupied in the meantime? As in the old *Hamlet*, of course—secretly, with intrigue and melancholy meditation, which to us seem not greatly to advance the business in hand (but must needs not too greatly advance it); and publicly, with a pretence of madness, which to us seems only to thwart it. But there these matters were,

91

superficially at least, less unplausible. There the delay, though like Hieronimo, in *The Spanish Tragedy*, the hero reproached himself for it, was attributed to the King's being difficult of access; and the feigned madness was represented as a means to reach him. These motives, like others that the dramatist found in his sources, he deliberately omitted (for a poor explanation only creates a need of explanation); and, as in *Othello* and *Macbeth*, he had recourse to manœuvring. In a play that bore such a title, and kept to the old story, he could not, without the plainest indication, which he has not provided, shake off the Senecan tradition;[1] and, prompted by his usual opportunism, he turned that tradition to account. Profiting by the familiarity of feigned madness as an artifice and a natural employment of the revenger at Court, not only in the old *Hamlet*, *The Spanish Tragedy*, and his own *Titus Andronicus*, but also in the legends of the elder Brutus at the Court of Tarquin, and of David at that of Achish,

---

[1] This point is what many critics wholly literary in their interests do not see. They are shocked and indignant at the old *Hamlet* (and *The Spanish Tragedy*) being spoken of in the same breath with Shakespeare's, and at the heroes at all resembling each other; and they more than intimate that such comparisons argue an insensibility in the speaker. They rush to the conclusion that he discerns little difference between them in quality, as well as kind. They do not realize that Shakespeare, writing for an audience, and a company, not for them, had not a free hand, if really he desired it; that since the audience remembered the old *Hamlet*, and other plays like it now on the stage, he, writing apparently only another *Hamlet*, must constantly remember the earlier too; and that his critics, to understand him, must as well. Writing for print and two thousand years after, Racine could make a *Phaedra* rather different from that of Euripides, and Goethe, a different *Iphigenia*; but *not* so different as this *Hamlet* expected by the critics of Shakespeare, when the other was not a dozen years old and recently was still on the stage. And still less do the critics realize that in keeping the story and character fairly intact lay the Elizabethan dramatist's advantage.

King of Gath—"And he changed his behaviour before them, and feigned himself mad in their hands"—he passed lightly, carrying his audience with him, over the reasons for it here:

> As I perchance hereafter shall think meet
> To put an antic disposition on,—

and by the time they are to see him again the hero has put it on already. The dramatist taking it as a matter of course, the audience would so take it; and not, like the critics, scratch their heads, and cunningly conclude (as a generation ago) that it is a "safety-valve", or (as nowadays) a case of "double consciousness", or any of the numerous other things it has been thought to be, and still less, that the man is crazy in reality. Thus, and by his subtler treatment and phrasing, he intensified an effect of contrast provided in the melodrama, similar (as we shall see) to that later invented for Othello, and, however improbable, too precious to be surrendered. And profiting by the familiarity of the rest of the intrigue—the baffling of the spies, the doubt of the ghost and the theatrical performance to satisfy it, the sparing of the King at his devotions, the killing of him (as is intended) behind the arras and the reproachful conference with his mother, the trip to England—the dramatist (to judge by the changes from Quarto I to Quarto II and the Folio) subdued, instead of emphasizing, its irrelevance, but accentuated and complicated its dangers; letting Hamlet perilously play the King's game (but beat him at it) as if it were his own, and, unlike Kyd's Hamlet, keep the secret of his revengeful purpose from his friends, his mother, and even from Horatio until near the end of the tragedy, and his plan to the very end.[1] Thus he heightened the suspense and mystery, imparted to the hero dignity, delicacy, and pathos, and threw the whole burden of motivation, or explanation, upon his self-reproaches.

§ 2

These, I cannot but think, are not meant to hurt him in our opinion, are merely to explain and justify the story. Here we are at the heart and core of the character; and even if Shakespeare had desired it, he could scarcely, on the contemporary stage, have introduced so fundamental an innovation as, in the place of a popular heroic revenger, a procrastinator, lost in thought and weak of will. Thereby he would have both disappointed and bewildered the company and audience he had undertaken to please. Rather, he kept Hamlet as he found him, only manipulating him more deftly. The audience were accustomed to the revenger beating about the bush but reproaching himself for it, and even being reproached by his confidants for it (as our Hamlet is not), without loss of prestige in their eyes. They knew Hieronimo, in *The Spanish Tragedy*; they knew the hero of Marston's *Antonio's Revenge* (1599–1600), and, in translation (as the authors did in the original), Seneca's Atreus, Medea, and Clytaemnestra, who, all of them, act and speak after much the same fashion. In effect the re-proaches are, as often in ancient and Renaissance soliloquy, exhortations, addressed by the character to himself. They motive the delay, not in the sense of grounding it in character, but of explaining it and bridging it over; they

[1] My *Hamlet* (1919), pp. 40–3. In Quarto I, the Queen is plainly told that her first husband was murdered, is requested to "assist me in revenge", and agrees to do her best.

motive it by reminding the audience that the main business
in hand, though retarded, is not lost to view. They provide an epical motive, if I may so call it—a *ficelle*, as
Mr Walkley[1] called it—rather than a dramatic one. In
all the instances above mentioned, as well as many others
in the Renaissance drama, reproaches beforehand for
failure to act do not discredit the hero or reveal an inner
flaw.[2] And, indeed, is not this simpler technique more in
keeping with the surface and common course of life? "Yea,
a man will pause", replies the Chorus to the complaint of
Sophocles' Electra against Hamlet's prototype, Orestes,
"on the verge of a great work". Who does not?

This is a case where what the character says of himself
in soliloquy, even though (as with both Sophocles and
Kyd) his confidants say it too, is not, according to the
usual expectation of the dramatist, to be taken at its face
value; or, we might better say, it is to be taken at that
and no more, being the sort of charge that Elizabethan
and ancient tragedy, concerned with ethical rather than
psychical defects, made no further account of. In those
days not everything in conduct was reduced to a psychological or sociological phenomenon, or was given an inner
meaning, even as it is not by ordinary people in ours; and,
in particular, not such a matter as the pausing or hesitating
which holds the situation, which prolongs the story. But,
it may be objected, the Elizabethan revenge plays being
crude affairs, all we can be sure of is that Shakespeare
could have profited by this tradition if he chose. In his
play the fact of the murder and the project of revenge are,
as we have seen, kept a secret; and this may be, apart from

---

[1] *Drama and Life* (1908), p. 151.
[2] See *Hamlet*, pp. 14–19 for the evidence.

the reasons above given, simply in order to spare the hero the blame of his friends. Yet what counts in drama is the positive; and Hamlet not only is never blamed or criticized but is esteemed and openly praised on every hand. If at any other time he had shown himself a procrastinator or a weakling, Horatio or Laertes, the King or the Queen could have said or hinted as much; and by the laws of dramatic technique, both in that day and in this, they were under a heavy necessity of saying it, and not the contrary, now. A villain who reveals his inner nature in soliloquy may conceal it from the world until the end; but Hamlet, if he has anything worth concealing, does so even beyond the end, while Fortinbras is declaring he would have made a kingly king. The tradition of the stage, then, the admiration of others, his own intrepid and precipitate activity on many occasions[1]—the effect of all these readily overcomes, certainly in those days (and for long after) overcame, that of the vague and conflicting charges which, in his noble solicitude, he brings against himself; and as Swinburne truly says, "A man whose natural temptation was to swerve, whose inborn inclination was to shrink and skulk aside from duty and from action, would hardly be the first and last person to suspect his own weakness, the one only unbiased judge and witness of sufficiently sharp-sighted candour and accuracy to estimate aright his poverty of nature and the malformation of his mind".[2] At least in drama—popular

[1] This is ordinarily interpreted as a spasmodic and frantic "compensation", and really part of his disease. Why then does Hamlet, in his ruminations, never remark upon the matter, or a little wonder at himself after killing the man behind the arras, or after his trip to England, above all after the prodigies of his prowess at the fencing-match? What an audience the critics have been presupposing at the Globe, or, for that matter, anywhere!

[2] *A Study of Shakespeare* (1895), p. 168.

Elizabethan drama, especially—he would not. Where else in Shakespeare is any secret, needful for the comprehension of the action, kept from the other characters—and really from the audience too!—for good and all?

And what of the reproaches in themselves? Here the dramatist is devious still, but to the same effect and tenor. There is, indeed, analysis, such as is not to be found in the other Elizabethan revenge plays; but with a "veiled confusion" that reminds one of Macbeth, yet more particularly of Iago. Both the Ancient and the Prince raise the question of this motive or that, but leave it unanswered. None of the motives at which Iago glances—the grievance in the matter of the promotion, or his lust for Desdemona, or his fancy that Othello or Cassio may have played him foul with Emilia—is sufficient for the vast villainy of his nature, as we already know it, and of his conduct, as we are about to know it; and his cool and cynical survey only indicts him the more deeply. He is a son of Belial, he is a limb of Satan. None of the motives which Hamlet considers—cowardice, melancholy, bestial oblivion, or thinking too precisely on the event—fits his noble nature, as we already know it, and his failure to act; and they fairly cancel one another. In the first soliloquy on the subject, "O what a rogue", he scornfully rejects the imputation of cowardice, afterwards, in ironical self-laceration, accepts it;[1] but he resolves upon the play. In the second, "How all occasions", he confesses that why he has delayed he "does not know"; but he resolves on bloody deeds. So similar a method with the two characters, and so dissimilar a result? But that is Shakespeare; and really, when the manner and spirit are allowed for, the result is

---

[1] Mr Clutton-Brock (*Shakespeare's Hamlet*, 1922), p. 121, takes the acceptance seriously—and the Prince sinks to the level of Parolles!

much the same. In one case the motives are made up; in the other they are sought. In one case the consideration is accompanied with a jest or a jeer; in the other with chidings and amends. But in both cases the audience is thrown back upon the introspective speaker[1]—already revealed to it as ignoble and hateful, or as noble and lovable. In one case, after each doubtful consideration, he holds his course with unabated zest; in the other, he changes it. But he does not change it again.

Only twice does Hamlet reproach himself—in the soliloquies just mentioned, at the end of the second act, and in the fourth scene of Act IV. The first is provoked by the example of the player's passion; the second, by the example of Fortinbras' martial activity. For the first there is the occasion of the hero's failure, so far, to do anything but feign madness and baffle hostile curiosity; for the second, to do anything but confirm the ghost's report. In either the reproaches arise naturally, and are needed to satisfy the audience, to point and justify the story. And that they are not needed afterwards is simply owing to the fact that, now, more than ever, Claudius takes the offensive—more than ever the game is his. Further explanations are not necessary, though no more than hitherto does Hamlet take the lead. But in life such a defect as the critics presume is not cured save by heroic measures, and in drama must not simply drop out of sight; it may drop out only if it be not momentous. To most critics the trip itself is an evasion, and the man is

[1] Or else into the arms of the critics; who for Iago, too, have found new motives, under the surface. For a fuller discussion of this character cf. *Shakespeare Studies*, pp. 382–90; and similar opinions, in a book of the same year, *Studies in the Contemporary Theatre*, pp. 77–8, by a critic who is not misled by philosophy and psychology, Mr John Palmer.

quite aimless now. Yet by Hamlet's previous remarks it is made abundantly clear that in going to England he is but turning the plan of the King and Rosencrantz and Guildenstern into his own—"I see a cherub that sees them", "'tis sport to have the enginer hoist with his own petar", etc.; and before and after his reappearance we learn that, by fingering his custodians' packet and boarding the Pirate, he has been as good as his word. What little he is suffered to say on the subject of his purpose thereafter is in a tone of cool and quiet confidence. The news, he says, will soon be out—

> It will be short; the interim is mine.
>
> I shall win at the odds.

And by the second soliloquy, about Fortinbras, before embarkation, added in Quarto II, Shakespeare shows more clearly than elsewhere, not, as has been thought, that Hamlet is of a procrastinating nature, but that his "tardiness" is not a sin or a disease, not a taint in the blood or a clot on the brain, but simply, as he and the ghost both say, a case of "forgetting", in other words, remissness, neglect, or "almost blunted purpose", for that Hamlet does not forget is plain as day. These are not damaging charges, and, for an ordinary audience like that expected, as at the Globe, have no necessary psychological significance. They serve for the narrative—so Edgar, Albany, and the rest "forget" King Lear and Cordelia, until she is hanged.[1] And now the neglect and delay are

---

[1] See below, Chap VI, p. 143. For other examples of "forgetting" (and the like) as a device of dramatic retardation, see *Hamlet*, pp. 17–19. It is worth noting that when the Ghost appears in the bedchamber, Hamlet is made to anticipate the rebuke. Here was the chance for speaking plainly to him and clearly to the audience, if they needed it. But the warrior-king, little concerned about his son's degeneracy, bids him comfort his mother.

7-2

over and done with: this soliloquy, with its final resolution, is there, if for nothing else, to show it; his conduct on the trip sets the seal upon it. It is unthinkable, otherwise, that the hero should never, in the two acts which follow, utter a word of complaint or self-reproach again. Evidently the soliloquy was put in, not as an indictment, but to make clear what was the trouble and end it. In that which closes Act II he has reproached himself with the duty undone, and, a doubt of the Ghost arising, he has resolved upon the play to catch the King. In this of Act IV he finds that still for some reason the duty is undone, and resolves on bloody deeds. "Thoughts", to be sure, is what he says; but that does not much matter, since these are thoughts that bring deeds in their trail. His words in both soliloquies are made good; both soliloquies are landmarks in the drama.

As psychology, certainly, the trouble is not made clear; yet, depending upon the success with which the character has already been enforced upon the audience, the dramatist avails himself of the familiar fact that the most practical person in the world may, sometime or other, say "I don't know why I haven't done that", only telling the truth. His friends press him no further, and Hamlet's friends in the theatre should not either. It is action, indeed, and little more, that he now engages in—checkmating the King, not killing him; but Shakespeare is again manœuvring, and making the best of a picturesque and exciting but irrational old plot. Here, as at the end of "O what a rogue", he is counting on the audience being, in their familiarity with the circuitous movement of revenge plays, satisfied with any action against the murderer. And only this defensive movement it must as yet be, for to resolve upon immediately killing him, and not kill him (as indeed by the requirements of the story, until the last act, he cannot) would make the Prince look more futile than ever.

In both cases it is action, not collapse; in both cases it is action which has to do with the King and with thwarting him; what is more, in both cases it is action which wholly satisfies the speaker himself. After the second soliloquy he complains of himself, questions himself, no more. And that the audience will observe, and are meant to observe, much more readily than the circumstance that the action is not the supreme one demanded. So the dramatist is enabled to content his audience, shield his hero, and still prolong his play.[1]

A mechanical matter again, which, however, should not surprise us in a crude old play rewritten. The effort to postpone the catastrophe is apparent in some of the greatest tragedies, like the *Oedipus*, apart from those which deal with revenge.

§ 3

In sum and substance, then, we have no right, as the critics ever since the days of Romanticism have been doing (and not only in this play but in most of the others), to interpret the character by way of the plot instead of at first hand. "To save the story, the dramatist lets the hero heap upon himself reproaches for his inaction; to save the character, he counteracts the effect of these by his own words, those of others, and the whole impression of his conduct."[2] And this pretence of action of the dramatist's is not a pretence of the character's. Shakespeare's evasion

[1] *Hamlet*, p. 25.   [2] *Shakespeare Studies*, p. 132.

of the revenge, or of plans for it, is not Hamlet's own. It has been demonstrated that his doubt of the Ghost is an honest doubt, that the sparing of the King at prayer is for the reason given; and there is no indication that anything else Hamlet does is more of an evasion than these.[1] On the stage, even more than in life, pretences and excuses should appear to be lugged in or snatched at, and evasions should look like evasions, as, indeed, for two centuries Hamlet's (if such they be) did not; and if the supreme dramatist's art in this matter is with our critics a success, with his audience, of which alone he was thinking, it was a failure! Certainly the hero's going off to England, which has been taken particularly ill, is least to be reckoned against him, as Swinburne insisted long ago:

The compulsory expedition of Hamlet to England, his dis-covery, by the way, of the plot laid against his life, his inter-ception of the King's letter and his forgery of a substitute for it against the lives of the King's agents, the ensuing adventure of the sea-fight, with Hamlet's daring act of hot-headed per-sonal intrepidity, his capture and subsequent release on terms giving no less patent proof of ready-witted courage and re-source than the attack had afforded of his physically impulsive and even impetuous hardihood—all this serves no purpose whatever but that of exhibiting the instant and almost un-scrupulous resolution of Hamlet's character in time of practical

[1] *Hamlet*, Chap. IV, "The Hero's Self-Deception"; for the doubt of the Ghost, pp. 47–51. That Hamlet should suspect the Ghost to be the devil is quite in accord with the orthodox Protestant opinion of the day. And that he should not be willing to send his victim to Heaven is in accord with the principles of the vendetta in tragedy and *novella* at the Renaissance, English and Continental; in Senecan tragedy; and even in the *Iliad*, as Hector wreaks himself on the body (and thus on the departed spirit) of Patroclus, and Achilles on that of Hector, mutilating it and refusing it burial. Neither motive could, without explicit indication, seem to the Elizabethan audience a pretext.

need. But for all that he has got by it, Shakespeare might too evidently have spared his pains; and for all this voice as of one crying in the wilderness, etc.[1]

The trip to England, like the doubt of the Ghost and the sparing of the King at prayer, is, though for the Elizabethan stage adequately motived, a deliberate prolongation of the situation, an artful postponement of the catastrophe, such as is, for that matter, to be found in Homer. Above we have noticed the kinship of Shakespeare's tragic method to the Greek; but at this point the ancient epics offer a better comparison than do the tragedies, since the latter, keeping to the unities, contain, save in retrospect, little in the way of story, or incident, which we are now discussing. In the *Iliad*, too, the principal characters must be kept alive and active, and (as far as may be) with reputation untarnished, till near the end; and this is done not only by the intervention of the deities (as we have seen), and many other expedients (such as a marksmanship whereby generally not a hero is hit but his comrade or charioteer or companion, on one hand, or as an extraordinary proficiency in dodging, on the other, not to mention the timely discovery of guest-friendship, the interposition of heralds, the coming of night, or the breaking of weapons) but also, even in the case of the most re-

---

[1] *Op. cit*, pp. 167–8. Shakespearean criticism is like the theological; and the great and formidable heretics, like Swinburne and Shaw, Walkley and Bridges, pass unscathed, untouched. Upon their want of perception there are no sarcasms, nor any strictures upon their opinions; though those of the last three, certainly, lay within the scope of Professor Herford's Sketch (1893–1923), and all four within that of Mr Clutton-Brock, as well as of the reviewers of books in which they are cited as authoritative. And, like other great heretics again, these are little heeded. Swinburne wrote the words in 1879.

doubtable warriors, save Achilles alone, by sudden, though not untimely, accesses of fear or promptings to "avoid fate". So Hector is saved on at least four several occasions,[1] not to mention those whereon he bows to the will of a god, yields to "a weakling heart" put within him, or gives way with all the host. Yet, unquestionably, he is no coward: by his tone and bearing, both his conduct and his reputation, he is to be judged. Neither is Odysseus one, in the later epic, nor Aeneas, in that to follow, amid their apprehensions, as, time and again, fate bids fair to overwhelm them. Moreover, these demonstrations, like the tears of Romeo, the lamentations of Troilus and Antony, the trepidations of Macbeth and his momentary refusal to fight Macduff, serve to mark and measure for us the tragic effect. So, at the end of Act I, does Hamlet's own outcry, "O cursed spite".

By his tone and bearing, likewise, and a conduct that is (if we be not cavilling) irreproachable, and a reputation that is stainless, is Hamlet to be judged. Even early in the play, as, in the soliloquy "O what a rogue", he looks forward to the Mousetrap, the tone is exactly the same that we have already noticed when he is looking forward to the fencing-match:

> I'll tent him to the quick; if he but blench,
> I know my course.

Such accents (unless I be utterly blind to the finer shades of expression, and deaf to the differences in rhythm of verse and speech) are not meant for those of irresolution

---

[1] *Iliad*, XI, 360; XIV, 408, XVII, 129; XXII, 136. In books VII and XXII Hector is afraid as Ajax and Achilles approach; in one case he would flee if he could, in the other he does.

or shiftiness, apathy or frailty;[1] and one's ear, not one's reason, is the best judge of Shakespeare's characters, as of Milton's likewise—not my ear, certainly, but Swinburne's, or Coleridge's (when he trusts it), yet even my own humble organ, for which the plastic dramatist wrote, I would boldly pit against the psychological ratiocinations of all the critics, which he never considered. In the form and fashion of Hamlet's speech there is no trace of uncertainty or fatuity, as there is no trace of suspiciousness or childishness, before he falls into the human devil's clutches, in Othello's. And after one's ear (for are we not at the theatre?) one's simple wits. In this case, as at the fencing-match and on the trip to England, and in the same way, he makes his previous words good; for he kills the man he thinks to be the King. What is plainer still, he thus makes good the words he had uttered as he withheld his hand from the fratricide a minute or so before. Here, indeed, is the "more horrid hent", to "trip him that his heels may kick at heaven", as he catches the murderer spying upon him. And these plain and tangible things, this record of promise and fulfilment, the audience would notice, and were meant to notice; and if few of them stopped to think that in keeping the great deed to the last he was like the heroes of all revenge tragedies they knew of, including Achilles, still, they were used to that, and would instinctively ap-

---

[1] *Hamlet*, pp. 38–9. Mr Clutton-Brock, indeed, finds (like others before him, I suppose) such qualities even in the cast of the hero's speech, and thinks that "he rambles on and on in a manner peculiar to himself among Shakespeare's characters" (p. 119), for example in the last soliloquy. If discursiveness were a test of irrelevance and irresolution in the text of Shakespeare, how many of his characters must needs suffer from the charge! The only place where Hamlet really is irrelevant is that which no psychological theory can justify, his discussion of theatrical art and business.

prove of it. It is both the traditional form and the natural procedure; obviously, the deed done, the tragedy is over. To interpret Hamlet's conduct against him to the point of taking his delay or his aversion for a psychical defect, is somewhat like taking Othello's trustfulness for mental paralysis or stupidity.

And really Hamlet's case is much the same as Othello's and Macbeth's; only, the material being different, and the old play intervening, the treatment must be a little different too. The Weird Sisters and the villain alike touch responsive chords; but in Hamlet the chord struck by the Ghost is the noblest within him, his love for his father. His vengeance, unlike the Moor's and unlike the regicide at Glamis, is a duty; and his aversion, unlike theirs, is not a virtue, although no flagrant fault. It serves to motive the circuitousness of the plot, and, when there is no more need of it, disappears. Not far from the end it vanishes, like Lear's irascibility and Macbeth's ambition shortly after the beginning. "That was what it was for", says Professor Mackail of the latter; "it has served its purpose, and is dropped."[1] A *ficelle*, again. Here it does not furnish the central tragic contrast of the play; that is provided by something equally un-psychological, the madness feigned. For Hamlet, not unlike the others in error, is, like Romeo, a victim of circumstances.

And of Fate, like his enemies. The tragedy is one of intrigue and irony, according to James Drake (1699), who wrote the first extended criticism:

The Criminals are not only brought to execution but they are taken in their own Toyls, their own Stratagems recoyl upon 'em, and they are involved themselves in that mischief and ruine which they had projected for Hamlet.[2]

[1] *Approach to Shakespeare* (1930), p. 22.   [2] *Allusion-Book*, II, 424–5.

The author of *Some Remarks* (1736) says something to the same effect, particularly in connection with Laertes and the Queen.

The Death of the Queen is particularly according to the strictest rules of Justice; for she loses her life by the villainy of the very Person who had been the Cause of all her Crimes.

p. 48.

And unlike most criticism of the tragedy since, this finds ample warrant in the text. There are Hamlet's own words about the enginer hoist with his own petar, and two crafts directly meeting; Laertes' about a woodcock to his own springe, and the poison tempered by the King; and Horatio's at the end, as he anticipates the story he is to tell. How strange that this bosom friend of his, neither through confession, on the one hand, nor observation, on the other, has any inkling of the Prince's mental malady; and it is not to deal with him alone, and not at all with his dilatoriness, *his* story "of carnal, bloody, and unnatural acts", "of deaths put on by cunning and forc'd cause",

> And, in this upshot, purposes mistook
> Fallen on the inventors' heads!

How strange that Horatio, like Fortinbras, misses the point of the tragedy! Indeed, so strange a drama (if such there be) would be inconceivable on the stage. But from these and the other frequent discussions, down to the time of the Scottish—untheatrical—Richardson and Mackenzie, as well as from the play's continual popularity, it is apparent that Shakespeare had not misjudged his theatrical public, contemporary or posthumous. These only delighted in the intrigue, circuitous but cunning, bloody but poetically "just", and took it for what he intended it to be, a story, not of Hamlet's procrastination—

that they would not have taken for a story!—but of a prolonged and artful struggle between him and the King. How far from the conception of present-day critics, that "Hamlet the man is *Hamlet* the play...the play itself, not a conflict of persons, but a conflict within the mind of Hamlet! The King and all the other persons of the play are almost passive spectators of the drama of Hamlet's mind, which they cannot understand",[1]—which is just the thing, indeed, that Hamlet is taking every convenient or inconvenient measure to prevent or hinder!

In all that period no fault was found in him. The author of *Some Remarks* thinks Shakespeare "should have contrived some good reason" for his delay, but—"so brave and careless of his own life"—discovers none. In all that period the play was, as the Earl of Shaftesbury, in 1711, justly recognized, "that piece of his which appears to have most affected English hearts, and has been oftenest acted of any which have come upon our stage"—something it could not have been if the leading character had been represented as a hesitant weakling, a psychopathic case. Once he was so represented, he gradually retreated from

---

[1] Clutton-Brock, p. 95, etc. The conception here is not absolutely representative of present-day criticism, but it is the logical outcome of the prevailing psychological distortion of the drama. The little book here cited, by a sensitive and brilliant critic, is in some respects also an instance of the modern critic going sadly astray without the guidance of a dramatic tradition. (cf. above, p. 31). Mr Clutton-Brock does not, as many literary critics do, neglect the text, but he seems unable to read it. The dramatic idiom which I speak of in the next paragraph is foreign to him—he reads the words, but in another sense. And yet when the book appeared—such is the state of Shakespeare scholarship when it is not a matter of dates and sources and glosses—it was generally acclaimed. In dealing with individual words and phrases the learned have a standard—the dramatist's meaning; in dealing with the play as a whole they have none.

the theatre, now a stranger to it; but before that he was probably, as he was in Germany indubitably, acted as a conquering hero. "So much the worse for those times", says even the historical-minded M. Legouis. But others may hesitate so lightly to reverse the verdict of two centuries of popular opinion and applause in the theatre, concerning a play written for the theatre, not published with the author's consent, and in both Quartos garbled, in favour of the judgment of Scotch professors and sentimentalists, Romantic poets and German philosophers, and present-day psychologists and psycho-analysts, exploring their own consciousness, in the study. Others still may have misgivings in acknowledging in a popular hero a tragic fault not discovered by a moral philosopher like Shaftesbury, or by neo-classical dramatists and critics, professionally on the alert for it, such as Nicholas Rowe, Fielding, Dennis, Tom Davies, Malone, Aaron Hill, Voltaire, and above all Johnson (who sought for it and was troubled by the lack of it), and first revealed to those who knew not and loved not the stage or its ways. The dramatic idiom[1] is not one of words and phrases merely, but of traditions and conventions; and why should not these successive generations of dramatists, actors, and spectators have far better understood it? A novel or a poem may, in its own time and after, be neglected because misunderstood; but criticism should be wary of finding this to be the case with an extraordinarily popular play by an expert playwright; and of stepping into the breach itself, when the idiom has grown unfamiliar, with an interpretation diametrically opposed.

[1] Cf. above, p. 108, note, and p. 49.

§ 4

There is not the usual refuge of muddled minds, a "middle ground". Hamlet, like Shylock and Falstaff, cannot conceivably be both what England for nearly two centuries with one consent took him for and also what critics take him for to-day, whether the later conception be thought to be intended or half intended, provided for "the judicious" of 1603 or of the nineteenth century and after. The two conceptions are antagonistic and incompatible, still more so than in the case of Shylock or Falstaff. Certainly Mr Dover Wilson's recent solution[1] for the Venetian usurer's is unsatisfactory: that, of the alternatives—"a great tragic figure, representative of the suffering Hebrew race", and "a comic character, of a devil in the likeness of an old Jew, a crafty, blood-thirsty villain crying out for revenge upon a decent Christian gentleman, and, at the last moment, hoist with his own petar"—"Shakespeare intended both". This the critic calls an example of "tragic balance"; but if he is echoing Coleridge's dictum cited above, there is no "reconcilement", either attempted or imaginable. The effect of the combination would be neither tragic nor comic, neither moral nor aesthetic, but chaotic or null. And the only acceptable mediation, I think, between the romantic conception of Shylock or Falstaff, and the earlier, lies in the recognition of the fact that the aesthetic ambiguity, in so far as it exists, was not intended, but is owing to the largeness of Shakespeare's sympathy, which would not suffer him, like Jonson or Molière, to keep sternly to a satirical

---

[1] *The Essential Shakespeare* (1932), p. 81.

rôle.[1] But like Mr Wilson's two-headed Shylock would be a Hamlet both morbid and healthy, weak and strong, irresolute and resolute, procrastinating and not procrastinating—contradictions, alike, in the world of fact, not of fiction, and not reconciled, as are those in Othello and Macbeth, by a conventional mechanism. And for me the balance in favour of the people and the stage, and against the critics and the study, is tipped decisively by three improbable implications of the current theory, already touched upon:

(1) That Shakespeare, rewriting in response to popular demand a Senecan revenge-play, should have kept the story and so much of its spirit and method, without clearly indicating this wholly different turn which he is supposed to give the character. To have done so, of course, would have disappointed the audience; *famam sequere* then held good even more than now; and as Mr Archer observes, "a hero must be (more or less) a hero, a villain (more or less) a villain, if accepted tradition so decrees it". But if, as the critics would have him, Shakespeare was a dramatic dissenter and iconoclast, a Bernard Shaw from Nature's womb untimely ripped; and moulded a Hamlet, and a Shylock, and a Falstaff, in defiance of tradition and expectation; why then he must each time have flown and flaunted his colours like the Irishman, without possible mistake. He must have expatiated in prefaces, and descanted in italics. He must have penned prologues at least. Actually, however, they don't think him a Shaw, but, in some vague way, a "genius", exalted above the

---

[1] See *Shakespeare Studies*, pp. 302–36 and the chapter on Falstaff. And see below, Chap. ix, pp. 157–8.

stage, tradition, and every obstacle (and therefore every means) of expression.

(2) That Shakespeare, designing innovation, should, on the other hand, have, out of the mouths of all the chief characters, praised the hero instead. If the dramatist had intended the flaw, he must by their comment have indicated it; as he does elsewhere, witness Othello[1] and Macbeth, Brutus, Antony, and Coriolanus. How amply is the much simpler mind of the Patrician general analysed, by friend and foe! That the hero must keep his secret does not matter—in drama still less than in life can he keep his character to himself. His failing, constitutional or newly developed, must have been made clear. Even by more difficult, modern dramatists, like Schiller in *Wallenstein*, and Ibsen in the *Wild Duck*, *Peer Gynt*, *The Master Builder*, and *Borkman*, apt critical comment upon it is found indispensable. But that, instead of criticism, he should have had nothing but praise and admiration poured upon him, is simply beyond my logical reach or aesthetic grasp. A problem-play and nobody aware of the problem, and in their admiration all of one accord?

For if this praise was mistaken, somehow, but unmistakably, the fact must be disclosed. Or if the subconscious (as has been thought) be here involved, through some prescience of the dramatist, why, even nowadays, when that entity is, as a notion, fairly familiar, it must, in the pages of Hervieu or O'Neill, whether by others or (subsequently) by the character himself, be explicitly recognized. How much the more *then*—when it wasn't and couldn't be! It scarcely matters that such psychology, of

[1] That is, as in Iago's dictum, which must be taken for granted. See above, p. 18.

the subconscious, not only unsupported by comment but running counter to it, is both a scientific and a dramatic anachronism: it is, what is worse, a solecism, and upsets the play.

And what can Shakespeare ever have meant by the dénouement? (Is it better that he should play the psychologist, or remain a dramatist, an artist?) There is the hero, outfencing Laertes, killing the King, wresting the cup out of Horatio's hand. There is Horatio, ready to die with the wounded Prince out of sheer admiration and devotion; and Fortinbras, burying him "like a soldier", and declaring he would have "proved most royally". And what is he himself thinking, now as his life-blood is ebbing? Not a thought has he for any fault or defect such as Othello reveals in his last words for his own.[1] Not a thought, either, for his triumph over it. "Done after all", is what, infallibly, he should say to himself, if he were the crippled, aspiring but despairing, spirit the critics have taken him to be. Dramatic art—even common human nature—would demand no less. If the tragedy be, as the critics maintain, internal, here, if nowhere else—and since nowhere else—the fact must come to light. The audience must be permitted to see it, if the other characters do not. But Hamlet's only interests now are in things external— his name, the news, his father's crown.

And if plain (though the noblest) English means anything, he is not, as Mr Clutton-Brock would have it, "insisting that all through the play he has been misexpressing himself";[2] and both has not a doubt, but has

---

[1] That is, according to the sophistical premise (see above, p. 18): "one that loved not wisely but too well", "one not easily jealous", etc.

[2] Pp. 38, 81, including the citation below.

every reason to believe, that Horatio can tell whatever he himself has left untold. Need I quote them, the dying but deathless words?

> O good Horatio, what a wounded name,
> Things standing thus unknown, shall live behind me!
> If thou didst ever hold me in thy heart,
> Absent thee from felicity awhile,
> And in this harsh world draw thy breath in pain,
> To tell my story.

"His anxiety cannot be merely that Horatio shall explain the external facts", declares the same critic, "...which could be done in a few words....Dying himself, his last desire is that Horatio shall set him right with the world. The play ends with this desire unfulfilled; and the entry of Fortinbras tells that it is over and that life remains for good commonplace people, such as Horatio, who certainly cannot explain Hamlet." Not that of Mr Clutton-Brock, certainly, who well says that Hamlet himself cannot explain him—a state of affairs (since nobody else can either) that is acceptable in life or in Freud, but not in any conceivable drama! Though (after forty more lines) the *play* is over, the *story* is not, and if Horatio's and Fortinbras' promises count for anything, the "unsatisfied" at once "shall hear" and Hamlet's desire be fulfilled. Any reader who rouses from his dogmatic slumber and remembers that he is not conning the text of James or construing that of Joyce, but (really) witnessing a stage-fit theatrical performance, is well enough aware why neither Hamlet nor Horatio is here at the end permitted to tell the audience what they, if not the Danes (before them) already know.

Thus there is less point, to be sure, to the words "in

this harsh world draw thy breath in pain ". The frail and
shrinking spirit of the accepted Hamlet has found the
world harsher than has ours. But why should *he* have
his story told, or have Horatio draw his breath in pain to
tell it? If all of it were to be told, surely he had rather
draw the veil—had rather let Horatio drain the cup. Fine
and reticent as he too must certainly be, he would not,
like a nineteenth-century Romantic poet, lay bare his
bleeding heart—exhibit his palsied will—to the curious
and unfeeling world. But for our Hamlet the story is only
not long enough, and he yearns to live a bit longer in the
telling of it by his friend. He is a lord of the Renaissance,
and loves name and fame. He dies young, dies in the
moment of his triumph, dies, as it must seem to others,
with all this blood on his head. This is his triple tragedy,
as Shakespeare, I think, intended it—a simpler and nobler,
possibly less interesting and piquant, conception than the
usual one, though one not less appealing. To some it may
even be more interesting because it seems to be more nearly
what Shakespeare intended—more like him and his age.

And why for the Prince, as for no one else in death, has
Shakespeare let the trumpets blare, the drums rattle, and
the cannon thunder, as not for Macbeth or Othello, who
were warriors, nor for Lear, who was a king? Why, even,
the final abrupt and energetic half-line,

Go bid the soldiers shoot,

instead of the couplet (as Mr Rylands points out[1]) in all
the other tragedies save *Timon of Athens* and *Coriolanus*,
if Hamlet were in the quality so unlike the other heroes
and least of all like these? As a stage-manager, and (of

[1] *Words and Poetry* (1928), p. 169.

all things!) as a metrist, Shakespeare misses the point of
his own play still more than as a dramatist, or than his
ill-instructed raisonneur, Horatio! But the line—the
salute—like the very Hamlet it was meant for, have long
since quitted the stage! The producers, like the theorists,
are not much troubled by the text.

(3) That Shakespeare should, in response to popular
demand, but in defiance of such a taste, have best of all
succeeded in satisfying both with what is an Elizabethan
anomaly. There are other Hamlets[1] in Elizabethan times;
but none of this modern complexion, and scarcely any,
for that matter, even to-day. An irresolute hero is too
unexhilarating a subject; but Hamlet, rightly interpreted, is (witness the past, whether on the stage or in the
closet!) not unexhilarating. Elizabethan tragedy is
romantic, heroic; and in the leading rôle there are no
weaklings, save historical kings like Richard II and
Edward II, these erring through sentimentality rather
than irresolution, and, anyway, not, like the Prince, held
up to our admiration. Both friend and foe speak plainly,
even in the presence. Only in comedy could such a
character have then been acceptable —it is his rank and
the dire consequences to the country that keep Richard
at times from being comic himself—and there Hamlet,
with the repeated pretexts and evasions attributed to
him, might have done well enough. These, if recognized
as such, could not then have been tragic; only by dint of
great precaution could they, on the stage, before an
uninstructed audience, be tragic even now. Mr Clutton-

---

[1] Apart from Kyd's Hieronimo and Marston's Antonio, Chapman's
Clermont (*Revenge of Bussy d'Ambois*, c. 1604), who delays the deed like
Hamlet, with no inner reason, for dramatic effect.

Brock has called the play a "tragedy of irrelevance"; which, on the Elizabethan or any other popular stage, would be, if anything, a contradiction in terms.

§ 5

What, now, of the present interpretation? Hamlet's madness, at least, is more nearly comprehensible. It is really feigned, not partly involuntary; and this is in keeping with Hamlet's words as he announces his intention, and with his perfect sanity when alone or with his friend. So, though less psychological, it is much more dramatic than if it were the presentation of a "disordered mind". It certainly is not a case of "double consciousness"; and the hero "misexpresses himself" only "under a compulsion" which he *does* understand, as, if simple and heedful, we also do.[1] For himself it offers present liberty and safety. For the drama it provides a contrast—the high-spirited Prince saying under a mask pretty much what he means (not ignominiously playing the friend or flatterer like the conspirators in *Julius Caesar*, the Greek Orestes plays, and the *Cinna* of Corneille[2]), and yet by no means betraying himself. Functionally, it is such a contrast as we have found in the other tragedies—between Othello jealous and noble, between Macbeth and his Lady engaged in murder and overwhelmed by conscience; but it is still more like the use of disguise, with its explicit ironies, as in *King Lear*, *As You Like It*, and *Twelfth Night*; indeed, in some other Eliza-

[1] Cf. Clutton-Brock, *op. cit.* Chap. II, *passim*, and p. 67: "misexpresses himself under a compulsion he does not understand".

[2] On a speech, II, i, Mornet remarks "Cinna devient odieux". And here in general there is the same objection to the active conspirator in the leading rôle. See below, p. 124.

117

bethan revenge plays, like Marston's *Malcontent*, it is by disguise replaced. In the matter of motivation, movement, and aesthetic result, however, *Othello* is still the best parallel. Without hesitation or struggle, without the clear presentation of processes or developments which would show how they arrived at this dire pass, the Moor, who lacks a jealous or a gullible nature, and the Dane, who has no sufficient reason to feign or dissemble, are nevertheless attended by all the authentic effects of tragedy, as, in the brothel scene of the one play and the nunnery scene of the other, they utter a mingled emotion, delight turned to anguish, love putting on the poisoned mask of bitterness or hate.[1]

Also, this playing of a part arouses suspense—we apprehend and dread the Prince's betrayal of his purpose. Not "double consciousness", of which the audience would comprehend nothing, it is a double situation, whereof they would comprehend the whole; the spies and his enemies are sounding the hero, and the hero them, and the limelight is not forever fixed on one melancholy figure's face and brain. Even in itself how much more acceptable is this madness as a ruse, though (on reflection) unplausible, than a madness half or wholly real, springing out of grief for a father's death and a mother's frailty— *that* is a thing more unplausible still! Hamlet has latterly been taken to be more fragile than Ophelia: she, within a day or so, fairly with her own eyes, had seen her lover lose his wits and kill her father. By some of the best critics[2] he is supposed to be suffering from "nervous shock", or "a wound in his mind", upon the Ghost's dis-

[1] My *Poets and Playwrights* (1930), p. 94.
[2] Bradley (pp. 113–28); Clutton-Brock, pp. 44, 45, 51, 75; and others. Cf. *Othello*, p. 32.

closures, as the Moorish general is supposed to be "stunned" upon the ensign's—heroes, both, in that robust and bloody age and drama! Words—mere breath—are too much for them! The ramparts and defences of their characters tumble down about them like the walls of Jericho. In this degenerate day, we who make no heroic pretensions, and never faced or wielded a weapon, are stouter and tougher than that; and better an unplausible though effective dramatic device than a mythical psychology! How much more acceptable, too, this scorn and mockery of the folly and corruption, weakness and treachery, which compass him about, from one who has no touch of it himself! In justice, our present-day Hamlet cannot, as he does, rebuke the frailty of the Queen. To many of the critics, to be sure, that is no drawback, for they would have the Prince infected and poisoned by the air about him, his environment. Sociology must have its innings too! But to the dramatist the moral and emotional aspect is uppermost; and the isolation—and opposition—of the youthful hero is part of his tragedy.

He is melancholy, however, owing to his grief for his father's death and his mother's inconstancy; and like the other Elizabethan revengers, who are melancholy also, but not diseased or really deranged, he is, at certain moments, even when not in the presence of his enemies (or, for no reason, in their presence), nervously excited and demonstrative—as after the disclosures of the Ghost and *The Murder of Gonzago*, and at Ophelia's funeral. These contradictory extremes of conduct were recognized in the Elizabethan accounts of melancholy, and (what is more important) were, just at this time, being presented on the stage, as in *The Malcontent* (*c.* 1600); and on these extraordinary occasions Hamlet acts more like Marston's

Malevole and Antonio (1599) than like any other of Shakespeare's characters. Whether the poet was at such moments under this influence, or merely that of the old play, or was even attempting an approach to a morbid psychology, cannot be determined. The first two instances of Hamlet's demonstrativeness, indeed, are by the occasion warranted; but his extravagant conduct at the funeral, where his enemies are present, seems to be the fruit of that Elizabethan infirmity of not knowing when to stop, or, as Dryden says, to "give over", treating the stage attraction of feigned madness, the late Mr Walkley observes, "for all it was worth",[1] as is done in *The Spanish Tragedy* and in Shakespeare's own *Titus Andronicus*. Why, though, undertake any explanation when Hamlet's own to Horatio contradicts his later one to Laertes himself?

By the present interpretation, then, some matters remain unexplained, but not the character as a whole. The difficulties seem to be owing to two hurried and ill-printed revisions of a crude old play and to the complicated theatrical conditions of the time. And whatever other mystery there is in the character is that of great but irregular art, not—begging the question—the mystery of life itself. It is not that of the still prevailing doctrine, literalism blent with mysticism, whereby we treat Shakespeare's characters as if they were real persons, whom we know but cannot explain—and therefore we are sure that we know them!—or whom we then freely psychologize and psycho-analyse, to so little artistic or scientific profit.[2]

[1] *Drama and Life* (1908): "Professor Bradley's Hamlet".
[2] I cannot enter into the subject again—I have discussed it several times before, but most fully in *Shakespeare Studies*, pp. 120–5.

Whatever may be thought of him, such an heroic but pathetic Hamlet as (in barest outline, simply for the situation) I have been presenting, has the advantage over the morbid one of being stage-fit and fairly intelligible, which the psychologists have never made him; and of being in keeping with the text, the times, and the dramatic tradition and theatrical favour of two centuries; and that outweighs, I take it, the critical tradition of a century and a half. Such a Hamlet, above all, is in keeping with the whole play, of which he is only an inseparable component, and with the nature of drama. He is part of the structure, upholding and upheld by the other parts; and some of the mystery in him is only that of plot, some of it, a matter of emotional effect, as his reticence and dignity. He is a dramatic figure, not a psychological study. And if as such he could be accepted as the real Hamlet, he would then, by that very fact, have the greatest advantage attainable, that of relieving a long since weary world—in a play written in comprehensible English, for the popular stage—of the necessity, every little season, of coping with another.

But he will not be accepted, as Swinburne foretold. He has no "tragic fault", which is demanded, though not by Aristotle. (But so he is like Othello, Romeo, even King Lear, as, for that matter, Orestes, Oedipus, Iphigeneia, and Antigone). His tragedy, then, in which the hero is not the cause of his own undoing, must needs be "a melodrama".[1] (But in that case the tragedies, where figure

---

[1] Clutton-Brock, p. 120. See above, pp. 42, 58, note, for the somewhat disputable ancient conception of the *hamartia*. If in life the Greeks considered motives less than we do, they did not in poetry ignore them; as appears, not only in Aeschylus and Sophocles, but in Aristotle himself, where he insists that the deed of horror should be done in ignorance (§ 14).

the Greek heroes just mentioned, must be melodramas too.) And what of all the maxims and allusions in modern English and German—certainly our Hamlet must stay as he is! Indeed, he has of late taken on our dress, super-fluously.

§ 6

Yet here again, as with Othello, have we, in thus dwelling on the chief character, attained to Shakespeare's point of view, which for understanding him is indispensable? Not quite, and still less than in Othello's case, I think. Is it not remarkable that Hamlet should not have been praised a little more to the purpose, as dauntless and resolute, instead of "sweet", "generous, and free from all contriving", eminent for his "noble mind", "the courtier's, soldier's, scholar's eye, tongue, sword", and for "the great love the general gender bear him"? How "irrelevant"—in the dramatist! Only Fortinbras' eulogy and martial honours come near to touching directly on the matter in question, and both the dramatist and his public seem less concerned about it than we and the critics have been; the hero's mettle sufficiently appearing when, despite his comrades, he follows the Ghost, braves and insults the King at *The Murder of Gonzago*, and, keeping his word at the end of the two great soliloquies, kills the man behind the arras, fingers the packet and boards the pirate, grapples with Laertes at the grave, and beats both him and the King, whether fencing or fighting, at the end. In *Othello*, a noble soul jealous is not a problem, indeed, but the situation: in *Hamlet*, a gallant spirit procrastinating is neither the one thing nor the other. Both dramatist and public are interested rather in his being loved by his friends and the people, and praised—never

122

belittled—by his enemies. In short, they are interested in him as an object of admiration and pity, not as a subject for study; and the admiration and pity is like that in *Othello* and *King Lear*, *Romeo and Juliet*, *Julius Caesar*, *Antony and Cleopatra*. As I have shown elsewhere[1] there is in Shakespeare, as not in the stricter drama of Racine or Ibsen, something like the Greek chorus, to serve both for interpretation and also for lyrical amplification and emphasis—a purpose that is by the Hamlet criticism thwarted, an effect that is undone.

And is it not remarkable that, however properly or improperly I may have interpreted them from the point of view of the hero's delay, the changes from Quarto I to Quarto II—the transpositions, additions, or suppressions, as in the monograph I have traced them[2]—should have tended not only to preserve Hamlet's dignity and attraction as a hero but still more to sharpen the suspense and deepen the mystery, and (what is better) heighten the emotional impression of the whole? The material for comparison is inadequate, the old play being lost and Quarto I being both garbled and curtailed in the reporting; but the above-mentioned effect is distinct and unmistakable as the result of the shifting of the nunnery scene (with the "To be or not to be" soliloquy) into the third act, the adding of the soliloquy "How all occasions", and the keeping of the King's guilt, and the hero's purpose, a secret from everybody but Horatio till late in the play, and his plan a secret from them all. The nunnery scene, coming as a climax to the King's probings or soundings, dismisses him to the Gonzago scene already alarmed and menacing, and

---

[1] *Poets and Playwrights*, pp. 68, 73, 75–6, 81, etc.
[2] Chap. III.

thus gains, for both itself and the other, in dramatic intensity; the soliloquy "How all occasions" not only assures the audience that the hero has not "forgotten" as he now disappears from the stage for his trip to England, but gives more pronounced emotional expression to his scheme of cunning to match cunning, intimated at the end of the closet scene, yet undisclosed; and while the disdaining of confidants and confederates (particularly in the case of his mother, though this, like the other changes, has only been reckoned against him) adds to his dignity and pathos, his reticence about his larger project, not only with Horatio but with the audience, serves to keep the latter anxiously surmising.

From plans, indeed, the dramatist shies away farther even than from the thought of revenge or the cause of the procrastination. Hamlet has none save for preliminaries, such as the feigned madness, the play, and the thwarting of the King in sending him to England—none for the deed itself. And it makes a particularly bad impression—I mean as a bit of reality, of course, not as art—that he produces no plan towards the end. Readers notice it, if spectators are too much engaged. Here Shakespeare is following his plot, no doubt, but doing better than that. The Prince is playing the King's game still, and reason for it. And if he loses in the dour psychological reader's respect he gains in the spectator's sympathy. For is it not a sorry business to scheme to catch a man and kill him? Setting traps, and by deceit and cajolery luring your victim into them, is not a hero's rôle. Agamemnon stepping blindly into the toils of his murderer, who is in the background, makes a better play by far than Orestes and Pylades, in the various versions, hunting the murderer's trail. When, the year before, Shakespeare tried his hand at such an intrigue, as he followed Plutarch in *Julius Caesar*, he by no means reached the summit of his art. Our sympathy goes out

to the poor victim, despite all. And in the emotional effect
and tragic quality of his catastrophe he here gains immeasurably
by letting the villain King still take the lead, and load his soul
with the whole burden of the slaughter. . . . And in going to his
death Hamlet keeps his reputation for astuteness as well as for
reckless valour by giving utterance to a premonition, and with
a smile defying it. Since he exhibits no plan, the reflective
reader may well, with Professor Bradley, shake his head at one
so ready to die "with a sacred duty still undone"; but the
unlettered audience is with him now more than ever, and joins
in the judgment of audiences long ago at the Globe. If their
point of view be taken (and what other are we entitled to take?)
Shakespeare here again at the end has not been portraying
the impotence of Hamlet's character, but has been handling a
dramatic material, hedged about with difficulties, with con-
summate tact. He is presenting, not so much—in all its
consistency—a character, as a highly emotional situation.[1]

It is upon an emotional situation, indeed, not a psychological problem (or even the avoidance of it) that, as in
Othello and in *Macbeth*, the dramatist throughout the play
focuses his, and consequently our, attention; and *that*, no
doubt, is why for two centuries it is "that piece which
appears to have most affected English hearts, and has
perhaps been oftenest acted of any which have come upon
our stage". It was a bloody, and in some respects for-
bidding, old story; and therefore the hero was now made
not merely not irresolute but, in both the presentation
and a repeated comment, sweet, generous, and amiable.
To the thinking of the more sentimental, or psychological
critics, ignorant of the Senecan revenge tradition and
unsympathetic with it, he was *therefore* made sweet but
irresolute, as the explanation of his inactivity. But the

[1] *Hamlet*, pp. 41–2, with some slight changes. See also, above, the conspirator's flattery, p. 117.

audiences of the seventeenth and eighteenth centuries, inured to the *vendetta*, with a supernatural warrant, entered readily into the spirit of the tragedy; and sympathized with Hamlet as he does *not* kill his uncle "when he is fit and season'd for his passage", which his father was not, *does* (he thinks) when he is "about some act that has no relish of salvation in it", in the Queen's closet, and does, with both blade and cup, at the end. They sympathized with him as did the readers of Homer for ages, until about this very time of the change regarding Hamlet, with Achilles, while he, likewise, carries his revenge upon Hector beyond the limits of life, even as the Trojan himself had done to Patroclus.[1] Such revenge, in the story, was the hero's filial duty and desire. Yet it being that, not as a reflection of the life of Shakespeare's day,[2] but only of their taste in story, his hero all the more needed to take the defensive, and thus be saved the stigma of revolting craft and cunning. Fate, and its ironical dispensations, must have played a big and obvious part in Kyd's melodrama; and Shakespeare, by his subtle treatment of the Ghost, created a supernatural atmosphere, which both lightens the load of responsibility on the hero's shoulders and accentuates the irony as, with apparently little inventing of his own, the stratagems recoil on the inventors' heads. But, above all, out of the necessary retardation of the catastrophe he contrived so cunningly as to secure the maximum of mystery and suspense.

In this matter, with his usual skilful opportunism, he turned defect to commodity. In his hands the hero, not

[1] See above, p. 102, note.

[2] As in Kyd's own, to be sure; and Kyd himself lets Hamlet play the defensive more than Saxo or Belleforest. But the elder dramatist was not so delicate as the later.

knowing why he dallies, and not showing us what he has up his sleeve, is a mystery himself. In his hands the King is more formidable and steadily more menacing; and we tremble for Hamlet stepping into the toils—as he appears meditating aloud in the nunnery scene, as he so readily sets out for England, as he so eagerly takes up with the proposal of a fencing-match. We are anxious even as he philosophizes upon death in the graveyard, mocks at Osric, and nobly apologizes to Laertes, seemingly without suspicion or precaution, though death, we are already aware, impends. In general, we are sympathetic, anxious, and excited, not analytic, impatient, or compassionate. It is somewhat the same effect as when Duncan enters the castle, and also (to speak of lesser matters) as when Sherlock smokes or reads. Even the soliloquies, we have seen, contribute to it, as the reproaches are heaped up, and action is resolved upon, though what, we know not; and in a manner the whole play, and like no other of Shakespeare's, from the second act—nay, from the first scene—on, is an accumulation of mystery and suspense, which is discharged at the Ghost's disclosures, at the Mousetrap entertainment, and, with greater volume and violence, at the other Mousetrap at the end.

And there, no doubt, lies the reason for the artillery: now cut by the stage managers, and coolly ignored or uncomfortably remembered by the critics,[1] it is an outward and sensuous emphasis upon what in itself is Shakespeare's

---

[1] Like a few others, Bulthaupt boldly takes Shakespeare to task for it; just as he does for Hamlet's being ready and fit to fight, and for his having been in continual practice. They quarrel with the creator because of his own creation! Professor Bradley, however, rises to the situation, and takes the booming and trumpeting accompaniment for part of " a strange harmony of discords "; and with his conception of the hero's character, certainly, it is discordant enough.

127

most crowded and explosive catastrophe. Elizabethan and Shakespearean tragedy, unlike the ancient, meant mortal retribution, even for the protagonist; and here retribution for four offenders, and the capital tragic deed itself, so long expected, come almost at once and together. Accompanying simply the accidental deed, and plotted death, of a psychical weakling or cripple, these thunders would be an outrageous mockery; even accompanying the deliberate deed and plotted death of a resolute hero, they are not, nowadays at least, eminently appropriate: but in a tragedy which is not of one man but of many, and is itself of more moment than any part of it, and, within one scene, piles catastrophe high upon climax, they break out properly enough (on a stage where such portentous noise was not uncommon or illegitimate), not only to mark and distinguish the palpable hits in the fencing-match, but, both there and after the eulogy, to signalize the importance of the scene as a whole. Where emotional effect is the chief concern, a greater weight of emphasis is, as in music, indispensable. And since this is the scene of scenes, where the masks are flung or torn away, the fell incensèd points of mighty opposites are bared and clash, and the energies checked and pent up from the beginning are let loose and recoil, why should not Shakespeare have now felt warranted in scoring heavily, *fortissimo tutti*? Moreover, it is a fine case of repeated *motif*, and (though a sort hitherto unnoticed) of irony. This demonstration at the duel is of the King's own staging; these are the same cannon, kettledrums, and trumpets that, from a distance, had signalized and celebrated the insolent "triumph of his pledge", at the height of his fratricidal prosperity, for the anxious watchers the winter night upon the Platform.

Here again he is to take his rouse, though, presently, not out of his own but his nephew's cup. And for him whose triumph (though disastrous) it is now, there must be, at the close, as a matter of course, another outburst, "the soldiers' music and the rites of war". *That* is not irony, it has not the true Greek and Elizabethan boomerang effect —*this* is for his enemies, in their poisoned cup and foils— nor is there such an effect to the eulogy of Fortinbras, though there have been critics honest and logical enough, but also insensitive enough, to say so. Cynical mockery in the accompaniment[1] is not in the vein of Shakespeare's drama; and it is not clearly enough indicated here for any. When Hamlet the man became *Hamlet* the play, the irony, like much else in it, was shifted; for after allegory and self-deception (along with the subconscious, nowadays), irony is the traditional chief contrivance or appliance whereby the critic who does not humbly accept the author's meaning forces upon him his own.

And there too—in the emotional effect—may lie the likeliest explanation of Hamlet's supposedly hysterical or irrelevant demeanour. Shakespeare is making the most of the opportunities which these great moments offer. After the prolonged tension of Act I, broken by the shock of his father's appearance and his disclosure of the

---

[1] Cf. my *Shakespeare Studies*, pp. 182–3. This is the Romantic, Fichtian irony, all-enveloping, all-engulfing—that of Schlegel, Tieck, and Heine; of Ibsen and Becque, Anatole France and Synge. Cf. also Babbitt, *Rousseau and Romanticism*, Chap. VII; and for the homeless, gipsy laughter of France and Synge, Stuart Sherman, *On Contemporary Literature*, Chap. VII. Nothing could be more alien than this last to the spirit of Shakespeare; as Mr Sherman would no doubt have granted, despite his treatment of Shakespeare as "our contemporary". The critics who treat Shakespeare as such always exempt him from the contemporary maladies or vices.

brother's crime, the Prince reacts in sportive merriment, somewhat like Byron and Leigh Hunt after burning Shelley's body at Viareggio;[1] and again, after the tension of Acts II and III, broken by the shock of the King's self-betrayal which recalls the night with the Ghost; but neither incident proves the hero morbid or abnormal. And in the graveyard Shakespeare simply overreaches himself. He has contrived admirably for a great scene, and till near the end such it is. We well know for whom the Clowns are digging as they argue and quibble, joke and sing; and when Hamlet wanders in, brooding upon life and death and their interchanges, we are concerned not only for the result upon him of the discovery but also for his safety. This feeling is heightened as the procession enters and the interment takes place. But when he and Laertes rant and leap into the grave, there can be no excuse for the Prince but the one, accommodated to the occasion, which the dramatist gives him afterwards; and for Laertes, none whatever. It is in keeping with Shakespeare's fairly musical method of developing emotional effect that he should at the great moments rise to great heights, and break into vast volume of utterance, as do not only Hamlet elsewhere, but Othello, Lear, and Macbeth. But this is a case, to use Dryden's phrase, of "his serious swelling degenerating into bombast", or into what the critic elsewhere calls the "roar of passion".

§ 7

Before the entry of the funeral procession, however, the scene is not only an admirable preparation for an explosion, but also a fine example, in detail, of this emotional rather

[1] Oliver Elton, *Sheaf of Papers*, p. 23.

than intellectual, musical rather than strictly dramatic, art. To dwell on it may make the distinction clearer. For the critics it is rather a demonstration in psychology. For them the frail youth is now wholly astray and adrift— still wider of the mark than when he allowed himself to be packed off to England—meditating, not acting, fatuously and futilely visiting graveyards, not warily seeking out his foe. But for the audience, to whom *Hamlet* the play is not Hamlet the man, and to whom, not secondary, psychological intentions, but primary, dramatic ones are most urgent and engaging, he is an object of greater interest than at any time hitherto. They are sympathetic and anxious, where the critics are analytic or impatient; just as when he came on the stage soliloquizing, and to talk with Ophelia, before the two crafty ones behind the arras. They know that this grave is hers; that the King and Laertes will soon be coming, both of them ready for him; and that this meditation upon death is under death's spread hand. But they are also expectant (as they are later, when he enters the fencing-match); for they recall the stirring news he wrote to Horatio, and the guarded threat in the missive which the King has read, recall that the Prince is no fool and has escaped before. Yet it is a quiet situation, and (now the musical effect also appears) an interval of calm and relaxation between the demonstrative and violent ones just before and after. It is "low tension", as Mr Bradley would say, after the high; but like the scene before the Castle in *Macbeth*, and unlike that of Hamlet discussing their art with the Players, it is evidently only the lull that comes before a storm. The silence tingles; the peace hides a menace; the audience half hold their breath. And it is a *piano* and *andante* movement, in

9-2

131

that range of rhythm, pitch, and volume which is more
extensive in the Shakespearean than in any other drama,
even the Greek:

> Shakespeare has not only verse at his command, as the
> modern dramatist generally has not, but he has also prose,
> and, in either, a far wider gamut to traverse. He is not
> meagrely restricted to what is conversational and plausible.
> He can be lofty, eloquent, lyrical, or fantastical, as well as
> simple or plain. He can take the highest notes as well as the
> low, the loudest as well as the soft and tender. And, as in a
> masterly orchestral composition, they then seem higher or
> lower, louder or softer, than they really are. They throw each
> other into relief—the comic does the tragic; the real, the ideal;
> the homely or humble, the grand or sublime. As we have seen,
> Shakespeare depicts passion fully and directly, in outcries or
> apostrophes, curses or ravings, lamentations or jubilations.
> But as Mr Granville-Barker has finely shown, he continually
> descends not only for its own sake, but for the contrast, to
> simple and lowly talk.[1]

That is true of all Shakespeare's greatest tragedies.
Sometimes the simplicity, or pathos, or comedy appears
alongside the high tragedy; as do the Fool's droll or pitiful
babblings in *King Lear*, or Iago's humour, or Hamlet's
ironical wit. But sometimes it comes as an interlude; as
do the scenes where Lear absent-mindedly guesses the
Fool's conundrums after the cursing of Goneril, and wakes
from his sleep under the eyes of Cordelia, or those where
Desdemona and Ophelia do their singing, or those where
the Porter opens the gate and Cleopatra receives the
basket. Of such as the last two is the scene now before us.
And in the last three alike not only does the action not
flag, because of the suspense we have already noticed, but

[1] *Poets and Playwrights*, pp. 119–20.

the comedy does not jar upon us. It is subdued, or modulated, by pathos and irony. As also in the other instances above noted, it blends with (and enlarges) the tragic harmony, through the ignorance or simplicity of those who produce it—the Grave-diggers, the Porter, the Country Fellow, and the Fool; or through the perception of it by those whom it touches—Hamlet, Lear, and Cleopatra; or (as here it does not) through the very consciousness of it on the part of those who produce it, as, though mollifying the effect of their cruelty, in keeping with it—Edmund, Richard, and Iago.

And not only do these comic scenes take a place in the whole tragic rhythm, but, though in prose—and not as prose merely, but as dramatic structure—they are rhythmical in themselves. There is a fine effect of repetition, as I have elsewhere shown, in the words of the Porter, the Country Fellow, and the Grave-diggers alike, to accentuate, not (as in Molière) the comedy, but the pathos, or the tragic irony, mingled with it. In the present scene the movement is more extended.

The First Clown, of whom Hamlet remarks as he enters,

Has this fellow no feeling of his business, that he sings at his grave-digging?

pipes up again, and throws out a skull. "That skull had a tongue in it and could sing once"—and Hamlet ponders on the "fine revolution"—the whirligig—of Nature. Again the Clown sings, this time the stanza which ends,

> O, a pit of clay for to be made
> For such a guest is meet,

and throws up another skull. The guest that is coming we know: but Hamlet can only sigh or smile, as he resumes:

133

"There's another. Why might not that be the skull of a lawyer? Where be his quiddits now, his quillets, his cases, his tenures, and his tricks?" And the Prince speculates further, on the vanity of property. "I will speak to this fellow", he then says. "Whose grave's this, sir?" The question gives us a start. "Mine, sir"; and the answer both startles and relieves us, as a flicker of mirth in the gloom. It fits the character, and is true enough: his attitude, like that of surgeon or undertaker, is professional— the grave is his. Thereupon he croaks out the two lines again, as unconscious of their import in this particular connection as the wind is of its wailing. For the delicate and tender Ophelia, how unmeet! "I think it be thine indeed, for thou liest in it"—and as they bandy words back and forth there is still more flickering of mirth or wit, as of fireflies, over Ophelia's grave.

> What man dost thou dig it for?
> For no man, sir.
> What woman, then?
> For none, neither.
> Who is to be buried in't?
> One that was a woman, sir; but, rest her
> soul, she's dead.

There for a third time the theme appears; but, though now more amply and clearly, and though more tenderly touched, in its full import it reaches only us in the theatre. "How absolute the knave is!" And then come the questions that bring up, in the reply, the subjects of Hamlet himself and his madness, and England, where he is supposed to be, and Denmark, where the Clown has been sexton, man and boy, thirty years. The Prince's past is summoned up before him—and the transition, though unexpressed, is obvious, and the suspense is thus heightened, as he queries, "How long will a man lie i' the earth ere he rot?" and, therewith, more personally and poignantly, the main theme of "revolution"—for this prose is as music—reappears. The Clown digs deeper, and puts in the Prince's hand the skull of still another, Yorick this time, whom he had known. This touches him more nearly—and what of the news in store? As he looks at it, the bone, he sighs and shudders, broods and muses, and in his mind's eye sees that of Alexander and that of Caesar, and then, in the course of Nature, the grotesque transformations and ignoble employments to which their dust, like that of all others, must submit. The movement, with its two kindred themes, has proceeded by way of questions, put to the Grave-digger, or to Horatio, or at large—answered, unanswered, or unanswerable; but now it winds up in a little coda of exclamation, and the prose passes over into a wail of rime.

Is Hamlet thinking of his own death as he ponders? That we now no more know than whether he has yet formed a plan, or still holds to his resolve, or why he has postponed action and has feigned madness—no more than whether Ophelia, who is presently borne in to this gaping grave, which has been Yorick's, and now fairly seems everybody's, has "wilfully" sought it, or how dear she is or has been to Hamlet, or why he hereupon comports himself so unbecomingly at her funeral. These are not mysteries of plot, which, rare in Shakespeare, must at last be cleared up; but of character, as in Iago, Macbeth, Antony, and Cleopatra. To the end of the scene (and well-nigh of the play) we are kept wondering; matters of motive and fact are veiled or neglected; our emotions are delicately or powerfully played upon, in varied, manifold, even musical fashion.[1] As the curtain falls we know all we need to know; but this scene, before the funeral, is one of *intermezzo* and *reverie* (though not of interruption) in the greater tragic movement, the more in keeping for being so impersonal, *un*psychological, with Hamlet less communicative than ever.

§ 8

The chapter on *Othello* ended on a note of satisfaction at discovering ourselves, apart from the psychology, in essential harmony with Coleridge and De Quincey; this on *Hamlet* (concerning which there has, for a century and a half, been little agreement save in unconscious disagreement with the dramatist) is to end on a like note at discovering ourselves in essential harmony with no less a critic and opponent than Mr Clutton-Brock. The wisest sayings of impressionistic critics, as of the academic and historical, are those let fall when they are, so to speak, off-duty, or (as Mr Clutton-Brock himself says, echoing Arnold) "disinterested", not reasoning and contending, but feeling and observing. In one of his posthumous essays, that "On Some Perversities of Criticism", written years after his own psychological and documentary

[1] Mr Murry (*Criterion*, Oct. 1931, p. 122) calls the scene "on the whole poor reading but good (though irrelevant) theatre". And in keeping with his notion that the whole play is an allegory (another instance!) of Shakespeare's difficulties as a dramatist, he calls Hamlet's discussion of their art with the actors "poor theatre but exciting reading". I greatly respect Mr Murry; but if Hamlet be an allegory, of this or any kind whatsoever —why then, I think, it does not much matter about the scenes. On the subject of allegory in Shakespeare see my article, "*The Tempest*", cited above. Elsewhere Mr Murry has himself complained of criticism so irresponsible. And see Mr Abercrombie and Mr Eastman above, in the "Dogmata Critica".

Hamlet, and, seemingly, in forgetfulness of it, I perceive, after this chapter was sent to the press, words fitter than my own to express its central purport:

> The greatest works of art, upon the experience of which principles ought to be based, are complex and highly organized, produced not for the lazy and conceited, but for those who will make an effort answering to the effort of the artist. Those who have experienced them fully know that such experience is rare and difficult, and no less wonderful when it comes. It consists in a sudden sense of the whole, by which all particular beauties are heightened and in which obscurities and defects vanish.... It proceeds as inevitably as a great tune; and, in fact, all great art, when fully experienced, is like music, meaning nothing outside itself, making a world of its own for us which must be seen or heard to be believed.[1]

Such a world it is in *Hamlet*, *Macbeth*, and *King Lear*, but above all in *Othello*, reminding us of the far-away world round about us, but holding us on its own enchanted ground, in its surcharged electrical atmosphere, enthralled, transported.

[1] *Essays on Literature and Life* (1926), pp. 203-4.

Chapter VI

KING LEAR

On *King Lear*, which, so far as the underplot is concerned, we have discussed already, we need not dwell. Criticism (as I take it) has not here gone so far astray. What attracted the dramatist was again a striking, but improbable, situation—that of a king, not in his dotage, undertaking to apportion his territory, according to their protestations of affection, among his three daughters, and, because of her laconic honesty, casting off his dearest, only to discover that the others were wholly false and she divinely true. Against the bidding of his heart he disowns her; and in the end his heart is broken by her death. Attempts, indeed, have not been wanting to motive this initial situation, to prove the postulate, to demonstrate what was assumed. Lear has been made out to be on the verge of madness already, like the author himself as he created him;[1] or tyrannical and "compact of vanity", as Stopford Brooke has it, to the point that the critic goes behind the returns, beyond the limits of the play, and bids us "just imagine what those two haughty, high-tempered, icy-minded, very intelligent women had suffered".[2] What can be the point of keeping the audience (and the daughters too) in the dark about such supposititious defects in his nature (and in Othello's, Hamlet's, and for the most part, Macbeth's), and also insisting (as in their case again) on

---

[1] J. Dover Wilson, *The Essential Shakespeare*, p. 120. See p. 85, note 2.
[2] *Ten More Plays of Shakespeare* (1913), pp. 206–7.

138

the admiration and devotion of his friends and retainers?
A stage-play is not a riddle, and Shakespeare's least of all.
"Das Geheimniss", says Goethe of them, "muss heraus,
und sollten es die Steine verkünden." And by both Brooke
and other critics much has been said of the "blindness"
of the old King to the inner nature of those about him;
just as there has been of Othello's and Emilia's, and as
there might have been of that of every other character
who has to do with Iago in the last-named tragedy, and
of Gloster, Edgar, and Albany in this, of the whole Court
at the Mousetrap in *Hamlet*, of Duncan and Banquo in
Macbeth (the latter of whom only suspects treason though
with every reason to make no doubt of it),[1] and of scores
of other clever people in Shakespeare's tragedies and
comedies alike when deception of any sort plays a part.
Here again what is structure is turned into psychology;
what is high-piled drama is flattened into biography, and
even autobiography. This is to blur the contrast, to with-
draw much of our admiration and sympathy from the
heroes and heroines and bestow it on the villains, to set
the structure awry, in brief, to rewrite the play. It will no
more do to be sympathizing with Goneril and Regan (or
counting upon their undiscoverable past) than (though
there is precedent for it!) with Iago, or with Claudius; and
the terrible violence of the old man before the first scene

[1] Professor Bradley (pp. 379–86) interprets it, not as blindness or stupidity,
to be sure, but (like Schlegel with Emilia) as criminal acquiescence. The
circumstances, the implications of the action, are, it must be granted, much
in the critic's favour; but in a play in compliment to King James, a stain, as
Quiller-Couch notices, would not have been put upon the name of his an-
cestor; and this is a case, as with Hamlet, of interpreting the character, indirectly, by the plot, instead of at first hand. The tone and spirit of Banquo
are manly, as are his overt deeds.

is over, is owing, undoubtedly, to the uncompromising attitude of Cordelia, in disgust with her sisters, and to the blunt interference of Kent, but primarily and mainly to the dramatic purpose of the dramatist. As Raleigh says of Cordelia, "if she had been perfectly tender and tactful [which, except with her sisters, she elsewhere always is] there would have been no play". Also there would have been none, as we have already seen,[1] had not Lear become so angry. For his wrath later he has justification, particularly as we remember that he is a king and a father in the older sense, with rights and privileges nowadays lapsed or ignored. But he less and less insists on these. His pride and wilfulness are broken, and he becomes, in the true meaning of the phrase, as a little child; his reason totters, but his sympathies are widened, his affections deepened. It is one of the beauties of the tragedy that he changes; but not so far as from a vain or irascible "despot" to the Lear we see with the Fool on the heath and with Cordelia when he has recovered her. Such a change would not even be psychology, and still less would it be that for coming about *within* the play.

The tragedy lies in the opposition between paternal love and filial ingratitude, and in the contrast between the old King's thoughts of the two whom he has cherished and of the one whom he has cast off. His casting her off and his yearning for her are not psychologically reconciled, as by vanity and anger they might have been, turning baffled love to hate. That would have greatly alienated the spectators' sympathy; as would a predisposition to jealousy in Othello, or a deranged or enfeebled spirit in Hamlet, or mere ambition in Macbeth. And his love and

[1] See above, p. 9.

the memory of the injury she has done him (or he has done her), having, like Othello's love and jealous hatred for Desdemona, *not* sprung from one root, as in a veritable human bosom, or in Racine or Ibsen, they would have, do not contend or struggle but are simply opposed. So they keep to the end; where, save in the Venetian tragedy, is presented the extremest case of irony in Shakespeare. There, however, it is better realized—

> Cold, cold, my girl,
> Even like thy chastity!

Moreover, the dramatist's concern for emotional effect again asserts itself, though at the expense of character; and is heightened by the aid of the artifices of music. The violence and variety of the passions call for a greater violence and variety of expression; and the orchestration that Mr Granville-Barker analyses is particularly fine and imposing. The device of repetition and echoing that we have found in the other great plays here takes a different form. The King's ravings, the Fool's babblings, and Gloster's murmurings offer continual opportunities to recall the errors and griefs of the past, one's own and others', new and old. In his feigned madness Edgar, as he whines,

> Through the sharp hawthorn blow the winds,

and, after an interval,

> Still through the hawthorn blows the cold wind,

is far better than any possible stage wind and tree. And instead of the spaced recurrence of a *leitmotiv*, as here, and in *Othello* and *Macbeth*, there is frequently also, in Lear's outcries, an immediate, hammering reiteration; as in

> O! let me not be mad, not mad, sweet heaven;
> Keep me in temper; I would not be mad.

> Hear, Nature, hear! dear goddess, hear!

> Howl, howl, howl, howl! O you are men of stones!

> Thou'lt come no more,
> Never, never, never, never, never.

And that is in keeping with the Titanic vehemence and impulsiveness of the play. Now though in this there is not necessarily any damage to character, certainly in the King's volcanic curses, apostrophes, and ravings the representative or mimetic function of dramatic art falls into abeyance; and at similar cost, but still greater profit, emotional effect is attained in the dénouement. There, indeed, the musical method is less apparent than in the *finale* of *Othello* or *Macbeth*. Lear and Cordelia have entered as captives and been sent to prison—to death, as the Queen (like the audience) expects, but, as the broken King imagines, only to the henceforth uninterrupted happiness of her company. At this point, if ever, in the fitness and the fullness of his speeches—

> No, no, no, no. Come let's away to prison...

and

> Upon such sacrifices, my Cordelia...

drama and lyric meet and merge. Speeches to be spoken, they are all but to be sung. But the King and his daughter then departing, a digression ensues. Albany, on entering, properly requires the captives of Edmund, who answers evasively, in a way that should be alarming; yet, for two hundred and fifteen lines, the attention of everybody on

the stage is occupied by other issues, urgent enough, but
to Albany and Edgar as nothing in comparison with the
fate of Cordelia and Lear. As mere matter of fact the
length of the delay makes little difference—Edmund's
word to the captain had been "instantly", and of a tragic
outcome we are anyway certain enough—but it makes
great difference to our emotions. Of the danger we are
four times incidentally reminded ere, Kent coming to bid
his King and master aye good-night, Albany cries,

> Great thing of us forgot!—

and all this, in order that we may be at the highest pitch
of anxiety when Lear enters with Cordelia dead, in his
arms. The postponement affords a climax, develops a
crescendo. As it disposes of the less important issues,
continually reminding us of the important, it throws the
scene which follows into the high relief which its supreme
momentousness demands. And thereby something of the
same damage is done to the psychological integrity of
Albany and Edgar as to that of Emilia and Banquo,
figures alike ancillary and subordinate. Relief, however, is
a sculptural expression; and it is of another art that we
must be thinking, though of tragedy still, and foremost,
as the old man totters in with his burden and his cry.

The climax is held—by another digression. The King,
broken and exhausted, presently wanders. He boasts
of killing the hangman; vaguely recognizing Kent, he
bids him "welcome hither." Albany now, not (as is
usual) at the end, takes order for the restoration of the
state. But passion recoils. "O, see, see!" and with that
piercing note tragedy again has sway:

> And my poor fool is hang'd. No, no, no life!...

Chapter VII

OTHER TRAGEDIES

S HAKESPEARE'S constructive method, even in the
four plays considered, is, though similar, not the same—
that is one of the high privileges and benefactions of his
genius—and in the others it differs more widely. In *Romeo
and Juliet*, which precedes the four, there is, indeed, a
striking contrast and opposition, between the families'
hatred and their children's love; but, as the dramatist has
not yet settled deep into the tragic vein, it is almost entirely external. Hatred contends with love even to its
overthrow, but not in the hearts of the lovers. There by
love hatred is supplanted, at once and for ever. In Shakespeare generally sexual love is not dramatized or analysed,
but is presented whole and unanimous, in healthy equilibrium. Indeed, as we have seen, *Othello*, *Cymbeline*, and
The Winter's Tale are only apparent exceptions. By a
contrivance, the passion is kept intact.

Of *Julius Caesar* and *Antony and Cleopatra* I have little
to say that I have not said already.[1] In the one, Brutus is,
though undoubtedly a patriot, not distinctly presented as
such; and is led by Cassius, whose rôle in this early stage
of the tragedy verges upon that of a villain, into conduct
from which, like Lear, Othello, Hamlet, and Macbeth, he is
averse. His admiration and affection for Caesar resist it.
But as with the heroes just mentioned, these motives are

[1] See *Shakespeare Studies* (1927), pp. 110–12, etc.; *Poets and Playwrights*,
(Chaps. I and III).

not clearly and openly pitted against others—his patriotism and republicanism, in this instance; his resolution, soon formed, does not change or waver; and the drama is not centred within him. He is a tragic figure, a noble soul in trouble. He unwillingly performs what he considers a duty (though he seems not clearly to understand it); and there too is a contrast, as also between the deed and its consequences. But the trouble is not laid bare: even as in the dramatist's greater work, the action is not the legitimate issue of the character.

In the other play, certainly one of the greatest, there is a contrast between character and conduct again, but without any mechanism to support it. There is, as Dryden regretted,[1] no intruding human or supernatural influence to assume some measure of the moral responsibility; and opportunities for an internal conflict or interaction are mostly ignored. In all the tragedies of Shakespeare there is much story; in all, the conflict is largely external—against Fate, persons, or circumstances; and here it is almost entirely so. There are changes in the hero's conduct, but there is less concern for the internal motivation of them than in any of the masterpieces with which we have been dealing. Antony's decision to marry Octavia comes about pretty much as a mere matter of diplomatic business; and his decision to desert her for Cleopatra, though prepared for by the predictions of Enobarbus (and the warnings of the soothsayer, which serve Antony for excuse), takes place almost as summarily. The whole psychological transition and transaction, which for Racine would have furnished forth the tragedy, stands undisclosed. It is not even presented as in Othello,

[1] See above, p. 64.

gradually though rapidly, in terms of mere poetry and drama. The story itself is too colossal and crowded to leave much room for that, and still less for analysis or debate; though there is a little of this, and something of oscillation, too, in the matter of Cleopatra's and Antony's jealousy, which, unlike Othello's, springs out of their own natures and their precarious connection. And the drama lies mainly in the imaginatively imposing spectacle of Antony's and Cleopatra's downfall—in their struggle for both power and love—before the relentless progress of Octavius.

Yet not wholly there; but also in the contrast between what the lovers are and what they do, and in what they are before and after their conduct changes. They too are nobler than they outwardly seem, and their lives are better than the record. Subject to no intrusion or temptation, committing their faults and giving way to jealousy of themselves, they cannot be so noble as Othello, Hamlet, and Lear, or excite so much sympathy as Macbeth; but the delights of them both are dolphin-like (as Cleopatra herself says of Antony's), above the element they live in, and so are their griefs as they meet their ends. Or, one might say, their love is greater than their natures: and as in a measure that may be the case in life, still more it may be in art. Either way, there is a right artistic effect. Of late, by two scholars, who seem to me more responsive to historical considerations than to the poetic and dramatic, Cleopatra has been declared inconsistent; but, in a woman's bosom, is not cowardice in battle quite compatible with a resolve upon suicide, prompted, not by sheer heroism and devotion, but also by pride and vanity, and by jealousy of Iras and rivalry with Caesar? Her decision was not quite fixed till she saw for sure that she was to be led in triumph; and her letting Thyreus kiss her hand, and her traffic with his master, were no treason, but the outcome of the bent for coquetry, intrigue, and bargaining native to her. The real difficulty is not that of an Egyptian queen a coward and a Thusnelda, a harlot and love's martyr, but that already indicated, of the lovers' devotion above their natures, or of their natures above their deeds. Yet it is a difficulty only as we consider literally and psychologically: their speech and manner, wherein the characters reside, are, as in Cleopatra's case I have elsewhere shown, consistent and identical if any are. Scholarship, unheeding—for it is often more arbitrary and irrelevant than impressionism, which at least begins with the aesthetic experience—nowadays proceeds with tradition (or influence) *this*, tradition *that*, as did the older school with *Recension A*, *Recension B*, whether the line of cleavage (which is the important thing) is, with the naked eye, perceptible or not.

In *Coriolanus*, likewise, which follows all these, there is, at the outset, no such constructive mechanism, or improbable and striking contrast between character and conduct, as we have been tracing. It is not myth or legend that Shakespeare is now adapting, but (as in the last two cases also) a history, and that penned by one among the most learned in human nature; and whether Plutarch's influence be at work or not, character and conduct are for once nearly identical. Again there is no villain or Fate; there is nothing even of the supernatural; and the "pity is worked up" to a still lesser height than in *Antony and Cleopatra* and *All for Love*. Here are the advantages, yet still more the disadvantages, of realism. There is analysis,

10-2

147

instead of the imaginative treatment of an emotional situation. The dominant passions, pride and love of glory, unlike Macbeth's ambition and loyalty, definitely appear, and are brought into conflict; and there is more of the later classical French method of fluctuation or oscillation than in Shakespeare is usual, when Coriolanus, under persuasion of his friends and his mother, twice overcomes his pride in order to stand for consul and twice gives way to it in doing so. As not in *Othello*, *Hamlet*, and *King Lear*, by the comments of friends and enemies the qualities which condition, and the motives which impel, a hero's action, are pretty clearly laid bare. His character, at last, is his destiny, and he bears the burden of this alone. Yet much as the critics say they like this in tragedy they do not, strange to remark, much like it here: one of them has, eccentrically, declared *Coriolanus* to be Shakespeare's greatest comedy. And though that is not good criticism, it has some justification, as it might have indeed if applied to situations in Ibsen where the prevailing trait repeatedly asserts itself.

The inner struggle, however, is not clearly presented, and appears mainly in deeds. Particularly is this so as the warrior enters upon his revenge: the dramatist here falls back upon his earlier method, and deliberately, violently, heightens the contrast. In Plutarch there is no word of *burning* the city, in which the hero was born, and his mother, wife, and child all dwell; or (for such several times seems to be the implication) of destroying them along with it. How did he come to this resolve? There is, in his long absence from the stage, no need of direct disclosure, which would alienate the audience; and of the resolve we learn only through his adversaries, who tremble before it, and his well-wishers, who endeavour to avert it. We have had signs of his love for his family and his dutifulness to his mother already, but in his speeches neither tie has been kept prominent; and Shakespeare has sought effects of terror and surprise at the cost of psychology, as these human feelings are ignored in the shaping of the resolve and then assert themselves to break it. He has, so far, in relation to his source, blackened the character of the Roman general, as he had done that of the Scottish thane, and the Venetian Ancient, and (for that matter) Richard III, King John, Angelo, Bertram, and Leontes, and despite not only psychology but, in some measure, Aristotle, making, in these instances, the personages *not* "nobler", but "the situations more intense". Thus he lets it be the worse for Rome when threatened, for Coriolanus when he yields, but, at either point, the better for the play.

Chapter VIII

COMEDY

Ever since the early days of Romanticism, critics have found a warrant for Shakespeare, as against the claims of classicism, legitimate or illegitimate, in the final words of the *Symposium*: "The chief thing which he [Aristodemus] remembered was Socrates insisting to the other two [Aristophanes and Agathon] that the genius of comedy was the same as that of tragedy, and that the writer of tragedy ought to be a writer of comedy also". But of this truth Shakespeare and the other great Elizabethans are not the only examples, whether within the single play or separately. Tirso, Lope, and Calderón, have each left us both tragedies and comedies and also tragedies containing comic elements; and not only Corneille and Racine, but even (as in some few cases we happen to know) the Greek tragic poets, wooed now and then the comic muse. And how much the two *genres* (like their counterparts in reality) have in common appears, on the one hand, from the fact that by masters like Shakespeare and Beaumont and the great Spaniards they are often made to blend felicitously; and, on the other, from the fact that by the serious-minded Romantic critics and actors the manifestly comic intentions of the author, whether Shakespeare or Molière, have, through mere shifting of the emphasis, been thwarted. *Behind* comedy there is always tragedy (indeed, since the days of Romantic irony, behind tragedy there is comedy); and sometimes by the author himself its shadow is permitted to fall upon the scene. I have else-where spoken of the violence done to Molière and the comic Shakespeare by putting in the foreground what with them is in the background—and that thing, quite literally, the actors have done on the stage with Malvolio, when teased in the dark room.[1] Congreve, too, has been mis-interpreted, his Lady Wishfort being made half tragic or pathetic in her affectation: the old or ugly we no longer have the heart to see mocked or flouted. Yet there are moments in his comedies when Mellefont and Cynthia, Valentine and Angelica sink back out of the merry mood, not into tragedy, to be sure, but into seriousness or wistfulness, and the laughter dwindles into a sigh. "Never let us know one another better," murmurs Angelica, "for the pleasure of a masquerade is done when we come to show our faces." And within the limits of comedy and tragedy both there is of course a still wider range of emotion and variety of tone in Shakespeare.

Nowadays, save by the mood and tone prevailing, and the happy or unhappy ending, the two *genres* are scarcely to be distinguished. In "drama" they are meant to coalesce. But in the Renaissance, as in ancient times, tragedy was more tragical, comedy more comical; and there was a difference also in the rank of the characters and the elevation of the style—distinctions which were, for the most part, observed by Shakespeare, though with greater latitude and (necessarily) greater skill. Yet with him, as at the Renaissance and in ancient times again, the

---

[1] By E. H. Sothern; cf. G. P. Baker, *Shakespeare as a Dramatist* (1907), p. 242. The Steward is meant to be heard, not seen. For the critical mis-interpretation, see *Shakespeare Studies*, chapters on Shylock and Falstaff, especially pp. 305–6, 303–9.

151

central situation and the development of it were, in both *genres*, essentially the same. In both there was a duplicity, or doubleness, of effect. As with the ancients, it was the result of human intrigue or supernatural disposition; and while at the Renaissance the plotter or mischief-maker of classical comedy often appeared in tragedy also, no fundamental change took place in the structure of either. The villain was simply a more enterprising and aggressive Fate. He deceived and inveigled, instead of foreordaining and foretelling; and he actually trod the stage. As with the ancients, in comedy as in tragedy, there was, for a complication, the same sort of misunderstanding that we have been considering; whether it arose from deception, slander, or playing a part, or from misapprehension, mistaken identity, or disguise. And then the effect was comic irony, instead of the tragic. The comedies of Plautus and Terence, of Shakespeare and Molière, are alike examples. Of disguise or mistaken identity, in the open or in the darkness of a rendezvous, and of hoaxes or practical jokes, there are instances in almost every comedy that Shakespeare penned. Of calumny credited there are, as we have already noticed, instances in *Much Ado*, *Cymbeline*, and *The Winter's Tale*; though these have, for the most part, effects not comic at all. The difference from those in tragedy lies only in the fact that they are not made so serious and are not so prolonged, the slander being but an episode. So far, however, the device serves the same constructive purpose. As in tragedy itself, this, like the others, produces compression and contrast.

Of such a structure as in *Othello*, however, Shakespeare has left us no comic parallel or counterpart. For that we must turn to Chapman, Marston, and Jonson, above all to

Volpone and *The Alchemist*, with their equivalent to the ancient intriguing slave. In Shakespeare's comedies, as we have observed, positive and deliberate deception is often treated seriously; and although merrily enough in such as *Love's Labour's Lost*, *Midsummer Night's Dream*, and *The Merry Wives*, it involves no continuous intrigue by a single person. The situation is not central. Of disguise and feigning, misunderstanding and mistaken identity, there is more; but, except in the borrowed and adapted *Comedy of Errors*, it too is rather episodic. And his comedies being medleys, both light and serious in tone, there is, for these devices, not so much need, or opportunity either, to provide a special effect of illusion.

They are more definitely external and recognizably traditional than verbal deception; and besides, there was in comedy then, and there is still, less of realistic rigour. Fantasy, exaggeration, and even distortion, are part of the comic programme. In so far as Shakespeare does endeavour to make these expedients plausible, it is mainly by shifting the scene, as from Athens by day to the Forest by night, in *The Midsummer Night's Dream*; or from England to Padua, in *The Taming of the Shrew*; or to the Forest of Arden, in *As You Like It*. There the thing might happen, we are readier to believe. Yet here is something of the same care as in the tragedies to keep the convention intact. Rosalind's disguise is impenetrable, not only to Orlando but to her father. And there is no reproach of stupidity attaching to these persons or to anyone else who fails to recognize the other disguised ladies in Romantic comedy, or the Duke in *Measure for Measure*, or Falstaff in *The Merry Wives*. Nor is there (as a result of the trick played upon them) to Benedick and Beatrice;

for from the outset we are made to see, despite their banter and wrangling, and indeed because of it, that they decidedly take to one another. In the case of verbal deception, on the other hand, for a purpose purely comic, as that practised by the Prince and Poins and by the Merry Wives upon Falstaff, or by Sir Toby and Maria upon Malvolio, such precautions to preserve the victim's reputation as we have taken notice of in *Othello*, would, by the very nature of the purpose, be much out of keeping. As in Plautus and Terence, Chapman and Jonson, this is a practical joke, a comic reprisal, or an exposure of folly; and openly the victim is made a butt or gull.

Chapter IX

TRAGEDY AND COMEDY TOGETHER

§ 1

COMEDY and tragedy, then, both were and are alike, as counterparts; and they must now at the close be viewed together, particularly in the light of to-day. In either *genre* this unpsychological method—by misrepresentation or misunderstanding—is, when rightly handled, and simply accepted, richer than the psychological in effect. In tragedy it is more tragic, in comedy more comic. And that is evident when at this point we compare the ancients, tragic and comic, or else Shakespeare and Molière, with those contemporary dramatists who derive the action more strictly from the character.

These are superficially more plausible but, other things being equal, fundamentally less potent, whether read or played. They move us less, by character or situation, by what is said or done. Their verisimilitude is greater, but their contrasts are weaker. The opposition lies less in what is human and emotional and more in what is intellectual—not so much at the centre of the play and more at the circumference. Mere character does not suffice for it. It must be eked out by ideas and problems. And there is a tragi-comic irony, not within the *Master Builder* or *Rosmersholm*, but encircling and engulfing it; and another irony, comic or fairly poignant, round about *Candida* or the *Well of the Saints*. Either appears less at the play than after it; and often as much in the stage direc-

155

tions as in the dialogue and action. The text, really, must
be both played and read.

And what is missing in modern tragedy and comedy
alike is, for the most part (naturally enough) what in
Shakespeare is now misapprehended. The bolder strokes
are wanting, the free spirit is not precipitated, and a new
and autonomous (though mimic) world is not conjured
into being, as it is by Shakespeare, Jonson, and Congreve,
Aristophanes and Molière. Often in the mere difference
of this from the actual world resides much of the comic
effect, as not of the tragic. For this is needed the illusion
of reality; for that, satire or burlesque, exaggeration or
transformation: but for neither, anything of a transcript.
Concerning the Restoration Comedy of Manners, Charles
Lamb was undoubtedly right. It is not "a veracious
picture of actual English manners and morals", but "a
world of itself, almost as much as fairy-land". A wand is
waved: and what is gross, licentious, and heartless is
transmuted by wit and mirth; or what is dark and seamy
slinks into the background, and only what is bright and
gay steps before us. The only defect in Lamb's criticism
is his failure constantly to remember what lurks behind.
"It is altogether a speculative scene of things, which has
no reference whatever to the world that is." If that were
so, this new world would not be funny—if by this merry
but significant "transposition and transformation" (as
Proust calls it) we were not, remotely, reminded of the
original, our own or others' practical and conjugal relations, in the world that is; though these, of course, must
not be thrust upon us, any more than Emilia's native
perspicacity in *Othello*, or they would break the charm.
Sometimes, indeed, Lamb does remember, as when in the

preceding essay, *On Some of the Old Actors*, he speaks of the "playful selections and specious combinations rather than strict metaphrases of nature". A *strict* metaphrase —a transcript—is, he implies, not art.

For the preservation of the comic illusion, as of the tragic, certain distinctions or manipulations have commonly been employed. As presented in their earlier intensity, and even as nowadays, the two illusions are mutually exclusive—only in the hands of the greatest masters does one with impunity encroach upon the other, and then it is in due subordination. In regular comedy, that is, the ancient and that of Jonson, Congreve, and Molière, noble passion or emotion is suppressed; even in the Romantic it is subdued; and for the purely comic effect in either, sympathy is unfavourable. In tragedy there are passion and emotion in abundance, to arouse both pity and fear. Indeed, the situation is deliberately manipulated to awaken sympathy otherwise not forthcoming; as in the case of Macbeth influenced by his lady and the Weird Sisters, and slaying the King behind the scenes, not on the boards. In comedy, on the other hand, the situation is manipulated so as to isolate the duped or cheated, the beaten or betrayed, only their follies being kept before us, the causes and extenuating circumstances ignored. Sir Toby, Maria, and the Clown tease the Steward and crack jokes at his expense under our eyes; Malvolio himself begs and wails in the dark, off-stage. Shylock is suffered to plead his injuries as a justification only in bloodthirsty triumph, craving a revenge which "betters the instruction", but to the cost of his own avarice, and compassed about by hatred, on the one hand, and by derision on the other. How they came to be what they are, what the world had done to them, is no more to be considered in the case of the Jew and the Steward in comedy than in that of the villains in tragedy. And so it is with awkward suitors and jealous husbands, stingy fathers and unsophisticated provincials, in Plautus and Terence, Congreve and Molière. Though not sympathetically or approvingly, we are ranged on the side of them that rob or cheat, like Tranio and Scapin; or boast, lie, and run away, like Falstaff, who, though he is guilty of all these misdemeanours, is funny. He is *not* so funny when with some Romantic critics we consider his hopeful youth and disappointed age, or take his misdoings for make-believe. Sometimes in Shakespeare, however, just as comedy encroaches upon tragedy, tragedy encroaches upon comedy, the isolation is incomplete and sympathy creeps in; and consequently the comic effect is not so consistent and emphatic as in Jonson, Molière, and Plautus. Shylock, as we have seen above, is a case. Falstaff, guilty of more venial offences, both the object and the inexhaustible fountain of mirth, enjoys plenary indulgence; and comedy and sympathy nearly merge.

Such is the mimic comic world—such are its order and economy—but what of the entrance to it? That, as to the tragic, has, by bold strokes and a precipitation, been often best, and certainly most expeditiously, effected. It has been by the avenue of these various devices of misunderstanding and deception, or of some particular assumption, all of which nowadays are (as threadbare or improbable, or both together) commonly considered taboo. In principle (though less in practice, as will appear) we grimly insist on what is both probable and original: such devices or assumptions, in Shakespeare and still more in the other

158

Elizabethans, who lack his authority, we, when we stop to consider, refuse to accept or fail to understand. There is the swindling in *Volpone*. "Cupidity goes with parsimony", cries William Archer as he turns away; "and who ever heard of avarice staking large sums on a problematical post-obit?" Yet even as mere matter of fact, whereon Mr Archer is here insisting, this logic of his is not that of common human nature. Often the most avaricious, though with a pang—and there, in reality itself, is a contrast and conflict of which Jonson fully avails himself—take to the highest play. Scotchmen I have known who, shortly after the close of the War, put as much as half their patrimony into paper German marks. And are not the French, the Italians, the Spanish, the very Hebrews, with whom parsimony is both the racial vice and the racial virtue, the most insatiate and inveterate gamblers? That fact of itself is enough to warrant, in a satirical comedy, whereof the scene is laid in a far-away and fantastic Venice, the assumption that cupidity may override parsimony, when the assumption is skilfully presented at the beginning. There, as in *King Lear* and the *Oedipus*, and according to the precept of Aristotle, is the place for the improbability—as a postulate, a basic premise. Mr Archer, so hard on Jonson, will not lay a finger on Shakespeare; but in *his* Venetian comedy, romantic instead of satiric, there are postulates still more improbable—that one friend should permit another to give his enemy his bond, valid in law, with a forfeiture of a pound of flesh of the creditor's own choosing; and that a young woman should, by the will of a sensible parent, be left at the mercy of the wooer cleverest at conundrums. These last assumptions, to be sure, lead to what is serious rather than comic or tragic; and it is the deception—the disguises, and the turning of the tables on Shylock—that more directly conduces to the comic. But all alike offer in comedy that advantage which we have noted in tragedy, an opportunity and warrant for the character to do and say what, quite of himself, or psychologically, he would not do or say. The avaricious dupes in *Volpone* enrich the swindler and impoverish themselves, gloating over the bright prospects for a timely inheritance from him, and so from the others; much as the miserly Harpagon is made to keep horses and servants, woo a beautiful young woman, and even give a banquet—that he may stint man, woman, and beast as he does it. And what they say is more finely incongruous still. Shylock complacently pities Launcelot as he lets him quit his service, both to spare his own and to help waste Bassanio's borrowed purse, not knowing that the lad is at this moment helping to cheat him out of both ducats and daughter—"The patch", he mutters, "is kind enough"; and so Sganarelle pities Valère, as, after giving him the ambiguous message from Isabelle, he watches him go off apparently heart-broken, but really elated—

Ce pauvre malheureux trop rempli d'amitié.

(The first-named comic effect has, in our sentimental times, been stifled or muffled.) And it is only from out of such premises of deception that proceed such dramatic conclusions as when Corvino in *Volpone* (who to outdo the doctor, reported to be competing with his daughter, offers up his own wife, of whom he has been savagely jealous) calls him, in a paroxysm of avarice, "*Wretch, Covetous wretch*"; or as when Ford, in *The Merry Wives*, impatient of uncertainty after the fatuous Falstaff's confidences and the trustful Page's assurances and misled by what he has

160

learned of the Merry Wives' intrigues, cries out, choosing
to be right though at a cuckold's cost, "I will prevent this,
detect my wife, be reveng'd on Falstaff, and *laugh at
Page*". By a more reasonable and more nearly normal
process of development, such a clash of contrast, and
consequent explosion of merriment, could scarcely, and
certainly less speedily, be attained.

§ 2

Therefore, strange to say, the best comic and tragic
writers are now falling back upon what is a modern and
contemporary equivalent of misunderstanding or deception, disguise or feigning, and the accompanying aside or
soliloquy; that is, appearances as the natural cloak over
reality (or all the reality there is), and consciousness itself
as a veil. The one is in Pirandello, the other in O'Neill and
the Vanguard. There is a prolonged contrast between
speech and thought, or between thought conscious and
half-conscious, as in the *Strange Interlude* and *The Adding-Machine*; there are actual masks, as in *The Great
God Brown*, and virtual ones, as in *Mourning Becomes
Electra*; and continually there are furtive, covert motives
—mothers hating daughters or jealous of sons, and fathers
hating sons and jealous of daughters—in opposition to the
honest, acknowledged ones. Or else, renouncing originality
and recurring to Ancient and Renaissance example, the
dramatists take to the old stories again, those of Greek
tragedy or the fabliaux, as do O'Neill and Synge. (The
Shakespeare critics are a little behind the times!) Even
before this, something of the duplicity of effect in *Othello*,
Hamlet, and *Macbeth* was secured by a modern destiny,
as heredity or family tradition, in plays such as *Rosmers-*

holm and *Ghosts*; and by a modern disguise, as the outer man masking the inner—what he or the world thinks he is, overlying what he is at heart—in plays such as *The Doll's House* and *Candida*. At bottom the methods, tragic or comic, ancient or modern, are the same. Fate and the *fallax servus*, Iago and Iachimo, Viola in a doublet and Hamlet playing mad, and the numerous varieties of fatality and double personality, unconscious deception and self-deception, in current use among us, all perform, with different degrees of verisimilitude and plausibility, of philosophic significance and emotional potency, one unchanging function.

And what is that? It is to make a situation rather than develop one, to frame a plot and precipitate an action, rather than to hold the mirror up to nature. It is to imitate life, not truly and faithfully, but, as with all art, in such a fashion—within the limits of medium and tradition, of the *mores* and the imagination—as to force us to think and feel. And this is the function of poetry itself— "to heighten consciousness", as Miss Sitwell says. For that effect in drama there must be irony and conflict, and therefore, contrast or parallel—and for any of these, in turn, there must be accumulation and compression. And for that effect at its simplest, in mere poetry, there must be metaphor.[1] The language of poetry, and particularly the greatest, is, unlike that of prose, charged as with electricity, "changeable" as silk. Of itself, life (or the plain statement) will not do. Even if it were different

[1] See Max Eastman, *The Literary Mind* (1931), p. 84, etc. For the surcharged quality of poetic language, carrying a meaning with many facets, but all within the compass of the poet's mind, not imparted by the modern reader's, see W. Empson, *Seven Types of Ambiguity* (1930), save where he is, now and then, led by his ingenuity astray.

and itself afforded such good situations as those of ancient myth or poetic invention, still it would not do. In great drama they would therefore have to be better, that is (again) improbable—though not *within* the drama, of course, even as such situations are not now. In tragedy and comedy both, life must be, as it has ever been, piled on life, or we have visited the theatre in vain.

And if not in vain, what then? To make us think and feel, to heighten and widen our consciousness, and nothing more? The Greeks, at their great period, the classical French, at theirs, strove in tragedy for a purgation, in comedy for a castigation, and in both for some measure of justice (not perfect or "poetic", but tragic or comic) in the lot meted out to men. Shakespeare and the moderns, whatever their efforts in either direction, fall much farther short of these. They have no religious philosophy like that of the ancients; and in tragedy they do not attain as the ancients did to any reassuring adjustment of human suffering to the will of Heaven. For faith is now broken; life is more intricate and mysterious: the notions not only of the benevolence of Heaven or Nature, but of the responsibility of man, are undermined.

How far this was with Shakespeare the case we cannot know, so little do his characters venture upon speculation, so seldom does he appear himself. Certainly he offers no solution to the problem. Though as a man a Christian and a Protestant, as a dramatist he has no theology or theodicy, no philosophy or "message". By some characters the gods are declared to be just; by others, to be unjust; and the only consolation in the presence of the bitter mystery is in patience, acceptance. Instead of the austere

11-2

but poignant serenity of Sophoclean tragedy at the end, there is, on the one hand, the spirit of quiet sorrow, on. the other, a practical concern for the punishment of the offenders and the restoration of the state; and the passionate symphony closes quietly, on a rest-tone. A note of reconciliation has, by Professors Dowden and Bradley, been discerned in the superiority of the character of his heroes and heroines to the fate which befalls them—in some distant reverberate intimation that what happens to Cordelia does not matter, all that matters is what she is— and the more senseless and monstrous her fate, the less does it concern her. But that idea is really a transcendental inference of the critics' own, not anything which finds a basis in the text.[1] There the beauty of the hero's and heroine's natures makes their tragic fate only the more lamentable, not irrelevant. Why should a dog, a horse, a rat have life, and *thou* no breath at all? Or, again, a note of reconciliation has been found in Shakespeare's sense of the dreaminess and unreality of life. But the most notable expression of this is on the lips of the bloodstained and unrepentant Macbeth and the blameless Prospero, in which cases, though for different reasons, it does no tragic service. Still less does Shakespeare put before us the terrestrial, social problems of an Ibsen or an Hervieu, which, however little in the solution they may purge our emotions, impart to the tragic spectacle a little meaning, though not much. And all that I can discover to alleviate our dismay when for the last time the curtain falls, is, apart from the life-giving spirit of poetry moving and hovering over the stage, the breadth and fairness, the exaltation and pity, in the presentation. (These are no matters of in-

[1] See my *Shakespeare Studies*, pp. 182–3 for the Hegelianism.

ference but of direct imaginative or emotional effect.)
There is no cynicism, no pessimism—the vision is too
clear and broad. Good and evil are not, as to-day, confused or merged, but are, as Croce says, "as light opposed
to darkness".[1] Evil is not negative or incidental; but
while under suffering it may grow worse, as in Macbeth,
good, on the other hand, may grow better, as in Lear.
And by evil good is not in the long run triumphed over or
overshadowed. If, on one side, there are Goneril, Regan,
and Cornwall, Edmund and Oswald; on the other, there
are Lear, Cordelia, and the Fool, Kent, Gloucester, Edgar,
Albany, and the true-hearted retainers and servants. If
many people do ill by those who have done well by them,
many others do well by those who have done ill by them.
The earth trembles; but the verities are unshaken, the
moral values and even the social sanctions are unbroken.
Justice is administered, not only, in the end, to the villains, but (though in a disproportionate measure) to the
hero and heroine. That is, the causal connection is observed and recognized; and in this tragedy too, once the
situation is attained, character becomes its own destiny.
The postulate once posited and granted in the case of
Othello and Macbeth, Hamlet and Lear, what befalls them
is for the most part brought upon them, in the natural
course of events, by themselves. And though our sympathies are elicited for them by artifice and manipulation;
and even in a measure for the villains also, as Richard and
Macbeth, Iago and Edmund, by endowing them with
"energy of intellect, dauntless versatility of daring, invin-
cible fertility of resource", and apparelling them (though
with a difference) like the heroes themselves in poetry,

[1] *Ariosto, Shakespeare, and Corneille*, p. 143 f.

or bejewelling them with wit and humour: yet, by all these claims upon our admiration our judgments are not weakened, nor are the issues confused. In fine, the poetically and dramatically transmuted and transformed material of life still retains life's proportions and values; and Shakespeare's tragedy wears the steadying, though not comforting, aspect of truth. We are made (and all along, as well as at the close) to feel deeply, and rightly, and to think sanely, if not to any definite ultimate purpose or upshot; and as by no other tragedy our consciousness is heightened, our imagination widened. There is, however, no piercing of the veil. Of Shakespeare the words of Hazlitt are truer than of Wordsworth: "He sees nothing loftier than human hopes; nothing deeper than the human heart". Philosophy, transcendentalism does not here apply. But when Professor Bradley reads with the same spirit as the author writ, he speaks admirably and to the purpose.

"Its final and total result", he says of King Lear, "is one in which pity and terror, carried perhaps to the extreme limits of art, are so blended with a sense of law and beauty that we feel at last, not depression and much less despair, but a consciousness of greatness in pain, and of solemnity in the mystery we cannot fathom."

Or perhaps Croce describes the result, though more dryly, more adequately:

He knows no other than the vigorous, passionate life upon earth, divided between joy and sorrow, with, around and above it, the shadow of a mystery.[1]

---

[1] In this paragraph I am somewhat indebted to Professor Frye, though at many points I differ with him.

Chapter X

CONCLUSION

Drama, therefore, if we are to judge of it from the foregoing, is no "document". (Not a social document,[1] of course—that question has not here arisen—but not even a "human" one.) Most of the misinterpretation of it, whether that of Shakespeare or of Aeschylus, has been more or less due to our taking it to be such. Whether as story or as character, it is, as Mr Bridges says of Shakespeare's alone, "not nature in the sense of being susceptible of the same analysis as that by which the assumptions of science would investigate nature";[2] and the tendency so to conceive of it is really the same spirit of literalism that prompted the sixteenth- and seventeenth-century critics to establish the canon of the unities—the consideration that they afford, not (as they do) a more compact and effective structure, but a greater *vraisemblance*. The human figures certainly are not, as a recent writer has declared them to be, "copied with little alteration from the population of the world"; and thank Heaven that they are not. Still less are they examples or illustrations of our psychology. But they are not always even perfect copies of the inner vision, that "higher reality" which, as Goethe

---

[1] For this—literature as not a record of the period—see my *Shakespeare Studies*, Chap. II, and *Modern Language Publications*, March, 1932, "Literature and Life Again".

[2] *Op. cit.* p. 328. In this passage I have always suspected some corruption —for Chaucer's scrivener the modern writer has both a printer and a typist— but the meaning is clear.

observes, great art represents. They are a compromise, an accommodation, a simplification, to suit the structure and particular conception of the whole. "The spirit of man cannot be satisfied but with truth, or at least verisimility", says Dryden, echoing Aristotle; but only verisimility is what art, drama, and more especially, among great drama, that of Shakespeare, bestow. It is not reality, or even perfect consistency, but an illusion, and, above all, an illusion whereby the spirit of man shall be moved. The greatest of dramatists is careful, not so much for the single character, as for the drama; indeed, he observes not so much the probabilities of the action, or the psychology of the character, as the psychology of the audience, for whom both action and character are framed. Writing hastily, but impetuously, to be played, not read, he seizes upon almost every means of imitation and opportunity for excitement which this large liberty affords. For everything he would give us, not only (in effect) life as we know it is, but (and far more) drama as we would have it be; yet remembers, no man so constantly, that the attention of his audience—the liberty of his art—has limits. Like all dramatists, he must have a situation; like all the greater dramatists, an intense one. He would, as would Dryden, "work up the pity to a greater height". Therefore, like them, he has, necessarily, had to start with premises or postulates, and provoke intrusions, human or superhuman, whereby the hero, still keeping our sympathy, can be put in a plight. And just because of the largeness of the undertaking—the whole story and an old one, many characters and situations, and times and places, not a few, and all the form and pressure, sound and colour, of existence—he has necessarily had—for consistency of illusion, swiftness of movement, and intensity of effect—to contrive more audaciously and variously, and (in turn) to make such amends or adjustments as he could, sometimes even by artifices which are scarcely art. He evades and hedges, he manœuvres and manipulates, he suppresses or obscures. But his most noble and effectual amends is positive—his poetry. The premise sets him free for it—*praecipitandus est liber spiritus*—and he walks not soberly afoot, like your philosopher, but flies. And Shakespeare is the greatest of dramatists because the illusion he offers is the widest and highest, the emotion he arouses the most irresistible and overwhelming.

By poetry, an imaginative conquest, he works the wonder—by rhythm and recurrence, acceleration and retardation, swelling and subsidence, and this in the structure, the rhetoric, or the metre; also (for obviously drama is not music) by the seizing and ordering of such thoughts and sentiments, such words and images, as belong together, though never together in this world before; and (above all) in the characters, by both the one process and the other—and who knows by what other besides?—as a vitalizing, differentiating power. His imitation is creation; what with us is dull and solid fact, assumes, still recognizable, the potency and liberty of fiction. So it is, in some measure, with the Greeks as well, and with Racine and Ibsen, who one and all are poets, yet not in such signal and pre-eminent measure, not to such dramatic—both airy and substantial—effect. They have less amends to make, but less resources wherewith to make them. Shakespeare's characters, more unmistakably than anyone else's, are, from the outset, given voices, accents, of their own—and not individual only, but beautiful—a fact which inveigles us, throughout the play, and even (witness the critics) afterwards, into accepting, not them only, but also the incredible things that they not infrequently do. They speak—like human beings, though none we know or hear of—*therefore* they are; and then, if for nothing else, their story is—" for the moment " —credible.

Appendix

Othello as a study in deception and self-deception.

DESPITE my intention to avoid controversy, I must, in connection with this one play, take notice of Mr Allardyce Nicoll's theories (*Hogarth Lectures*, 1927). They are, of course, not in the same category with Mr Knight's (*v. supra*, p. 31), proceeding from the pen of one who has a far wider knowledge and finer experience of the drama. Yet he has something of the same indifference to the dramatist's purpose, and to the traditions and technique whereby it is expressed. He reads this tragedy as if it were a problem-play, in the style of Hervieu. For him both Othello and Desdemona are stupid—"lack of intellect" is the tactful phrase he uses—though Emilia is left out of consideration; and the tragedy is a study in deception and self-deception. These two processes are exemplified in not only Iago but Othello and Desdemona —again Emilia is ignored—and the tragedy becomes another, an Elizabethan, *Connais-toi* (1909). The hero deceives himself in thinking he is not jealous or inflammable by nature; Iago deceives himself in thinking he can play with fire in the hero's neighbourhood without starting a conflagration. How, then, does Mr Nicoll dispose of the unanimity of Desdemona, Lodovico, and "our full senate"—are they self-deceivers all? And as for Iago not intending anything so serious at the outset, surely the

171

sentiment in the last line of his first soliloquy, at the end of the first Act, where first he speaks his mind—

> Hell and Night
> Must bring this monstrous birth to the world's light,

is definite and devilish enough. Only the ways and means are still undetermined (or undisclosed), though that is quite in keeping with a murderous purpose and also (what Mr Nicoll too often forgets) dramatic technique and effect. His Iago, a case of perverted idealism and inferiority-complex, is (as he will no doubt gladly admit) Bradley's monistic one; instead of Shakespeare's dualistic one (if really philosophical ideas should here be considered), and (what is more to the point), instead of a stage figure, both tragic and comic, developed, to perfection, out of the Vice and the Machiavel—the "devil", "demi-devil", that Othello calls him at the end.

Error, in Shakespeare criticism at least, is never killed, but this of the popular Elizabethan's penning plays with central ideas was scotched by R. G. White two generations ago; and surely Mr Nicoll knows as well as I that deception, whereby Shakespeare, like all the rest of the Renaissance, constructed his plays, could not, without very explicit indication, be made the central idea in one of them. If such a central idea be in *Othello*, then it is, as Mr Masefield thinks, in most of the others, and therefore has no significance or value in any (cf. my *Shakespeare Studies*, p. 101). As for self-deception, a process little represented by Shakespeare, and then so clearly and immediately recognized by the character himself that it scarcely deserves the name, see *ibid.*, pp. 126–41; and for it as a device continually, for the critic's own purposes, imposed upon him, cf. above, p. 129. How clearly even the true variety, the subconscious, is marked in Ibsen's *Wild Duck*, and recognized by the characters, after the fact, in *Connais-toi*, plays written for a modern and cultivated audience, familiar with the notion, not the Elizabethan promiscuous one at the Globe!

NOTE B

Othello's last speech

Mr T. S. ELIOT takes this final phase of the hero psychologically—he "is cheering himself up. He is endeavouring to escape reality, . . . turning himself into a pathetic figure, by adopting an *aesthetic* rather than a moral attitude, dramatising himself against his environment." Something the same the critic finds in Hamlet, Antony, and Coriolanus, as they face the end. Are these, then, now only playing a part, like a Thackeray fribble or coquette? As I have shown elsewhere[1] this is a self-descriptive method, as in Chapman and Marston, and in Seneca before them, and not merely at the end of a play, nor merely in connection with the hero: if taken as a bit of self-consciousness, it much troubles the noble and heroic impression. But the main matter in question is one of rhythm; Othello, obscured, must shine forth again; maddened, he must come to his senses; stained with a hideous crime, he must see and show himself as he is. And even as dramatic psychology—that is, such as does not press and peer behind drama and poetry—the speech is finely appropriate. After such an experience and such depths of

[1] *Poets and Playwrights*, p. 59 and note.

despair Othello must, in sheer reaction and relapse, think a little well of himself. It is one of the glories of Shakespeare that, unlike the French classicists, he recognizes the limits of human nature: it is also one of the sources of his dramatic effect. Both the one truth and the other are exemplified also at the end of Lear.

NOTE C (to be added to § 2, p. 64)
Chaucer's *Troilus and Cressida*

CHAUCER'S *Troilus and Cressida* is a more sophisticated example of the same art. Both human intrigue and supernatural disposition—not only Pandarus but destiny or the god of love—play a part in the fortunes of the hero and the heroine; thus, as in the other instances considered, they give body and momentum to the story, and in his case lighten the charge of folly against him, in hers that of unfaithfulness. Cressida is the character more in dispute; and, like Shakespeare's chief tragic heroes, in that position she will continue to be so long as she is taken merely for a specimen of psychology and her story for the image of life. Is she a dupe, a schemer, or a riddle? She is none of these (though perhaps a little of each), but a clever, charming, tender-hearted woman, who in her frailty receives our sympathy as she does the poet's. And it is particularly by reason of the supernatural—unnatural —influence upon her conduct that she receives this sympathy so freely. For the conduct of Manon Lescaut there is, and, in the circumstances, could be, no such explanation or excuse.

Index

(This index of proper names is designed to supplement the table of contents. Characters seldom mentioned are listed under the play, plays seldom mentioned under the author. The critics cited in the "Dogmata" are not included.)